56

p. 217 → pagination

pp. 252, 3, 5, 7, 1 – index

pp. 101–7 – chapter heading.

p. 215 – word omitted.

p. 194 – editing change

p. 223 – de-italicize

p. 210 – de-italicize

p. 14 – double period.

p. 239 – comma replaces '—'

p. 193 – remove gap

p. 241 – re-word

p. 187 – inv. commas to be deleted

p. 105 – insert comma

<, > : change to angular brackets, ⟨, ⟩, on following

pages :

37 (fig 3-3)	126 (fig 9-8)
46 (fig 4-2)	125 (fig 9-7)
47	123 (fig 9-6)
44 (fig 4-1)	180 (fig 12-3)
67 (fig 5-3)	181 (fig 12-4)
72 (fig 6-1)	179 (fig 12-2)
77 (fig. 6-2)	
83 (fig 6-3)	

---

p. 207 – refine graph – curve C.

p. 205 – refine graph (fig 13-3)

p. 209 – refine graph.

AN INSTITUTIONAL INVESTOR PUBLICATION

OPTIONS HEDGING & ARBITRAGE

SIMON EADES

PROBUS PUBLISHING COMPANY
Chicago, Illinois

Library of Congress Cataloging in Publication Data Available

ISBN 1-55738-256-5

Printed in the United States of America

BB

1 2 3 4 5 6 7 8 9 0

Contents

Preface

The evolution of modern option theory in the early 1970s brought not only a means by which analysts could rationally value a class of relatively arcane and (at that time) obscure financial instruments, but also a tool of enormous power, versatility and potential application. For option theory suggests a means by which to analyze the formal characteristics of the risk-reward relationship which lies at the heart of all financial decision-making. Option theory is thus of real relevance to financial managers and aspiring financial managers, whether or not they have any direct involvement with the trading of options themselves.

This book is designed to set forth the principles embodied in option theory in a manner as accessible as possible. And accessibility is key, because the complex mathematics entailed in the derivation of option pricing formulae tend to deter many of those who stand to benefit most from their use and application. So while Chapter 13, for example, contains a derivation of the somewhat complex continuous-time option pricing model, it is included largely to ensure completeness. The purpose of this book is to convey to the moderately numerate manager and student a clear grasp of the principles from which option theory derives, as well as a clear sense of the importance and relevance of those principles in financial decision-making beyond the singular arena of the options markets.

The book can be divided into four parts. The first part—Chapters 1 through 6—concerns discounted cash-flow (DCF) analysis and forward and arbitrage pricing methodology. As well as being important in their own right, DCF analysis, the arbitrage pricing method and other techniques covered in these early chapters reappear when we come to the derivations of the more advanced valuation techniques covered later in the book. The second part—Chapters 7 through 11—introduces elementary risk-reward analysis, options, warrants and convertible debentures, and the basics of the modern approach to their analysis and valuation. In part three—Chapters 12 and 13—we derive the binomial option pricing model and its continuous-time limiting case, sometimes known as the Black-Scholes model, after those who first derived it in the early 1970s. Finally, in part four (Chapters 14, 15 and 16), we apply the principles and insights evolved in the earlier parts of the book to the design and application of arbitrage strategies and capital financing decisions. We examine the potential pitfalls of over-reliance upon the apparent objectivity and utility of option pricing theory, and also examine how the theory embodies certain important assumptions which though reasonable can, if not made explicit, tempt the arbitrageur into potentially damaging strategies and positions.

A final note needs to be added: this book is designed to elucidate *principles* of pricing and arbitrage. Omitted from the analysis throughout is any consideration of the effects of taxes or other potential costs, such as commissions. These effects are so variable, and the theory is so readily adapted to their accommodation, that their inclusion here would be more obfuscating than illuminating.

The ideas presented in the following pages have evolved and been fashioned under the influence of friends, colleagues and teachers too numerous to mention individually. Their influence, indulgence and encouragement has been much appreciated. Finally, this book is dedicated to P.H.E. and (in alphabetical order) Alex, Emma, George, James, Katie and Mimi, with best wishes for the future.

Simon Eades

Chapter 1

1

Setting the Scene

In the wake of the U.S. stock market crash of October 19th, 1987, the attention of the market, its regulators and the investing public was particularly focused on the impact of high-volume, computer program-driven trading strategies and their role in increasing market volatility. People asked how it was that the crash (or "dislocation," as it was euphemistically described by some commentators) could occur in an era in which sophisticated quantitative techniques had been developed and were in use in connection with the valuation of securities. To many, the precipitous drop in the market suggested that the practice of investing and securities valuation could not, after all, be reduced to the status of a strict science in which decision-making is optimized by the discovery and application of principles which have the force of natural law. In contrast to the sweeping regulatory changes that followed the '29 crash, the major legacy of the '87 debacle appears to be the idea that securities valuation (and management in general) is, after all, in large part art.

This book is designed to throw light on the principles of sound and rational pricing in securities markets by drawing out the formal relationships between the variables of which soundness is a function. But, importantly, the book is also intended to put those relationships (and the formulae which embody them) into their proper logical context. And by doing this it will be shown why quantitative methods are helpful but never sufficient to derive rational securities values. It will be shown that, as a matter of logic, subjectivity can never be wholly eliminated from the valuation process. The importance of this fact lies not in its relevance to any debate over whether investing is an art or a science, but in the insights it affords into the risks entailed in the management of any business involving the purchase or sale—including the sale as issuer—of securities.

It particularly should be noted that what follows neglects mention of what is perhaps the single most important (and most difficult to analyze) influence on securities prices—human psychology. Periods of market volatility—such as the '87 crash—often have a great deal to do with psychology and very little to do with financial theory. In most cases, no complete explanation can be given as to why a particular security was valued at such-and-such one day and a fraction of such-and-such the next without involving a reference to human psychology. Against this background, it might reasonably be asked why a theory of rational securities pricing is of interest; why would an investor not do better to study psychology than finance?

The reason is both simple and important. It is that a theory of rational securities pricing will tell us *something about a security* itself (viz, on the basis of certain assumptions, what it is worth), while a theory of investor psychology will tell us *something about an investor.* In a world in which only psychology was studied we would have no means by which to relate the *market* value of any security to its *intrinsic* value. And it seems almost self-evidently true that it should be desirable to have securities markets in which market values reflect intrinsic values as closely as possible.

Given, then, that pricing theory is desirable, the question arises whether it makes sense to talk of *a* theory of rational securities pricing, rather than, for example, a bond pricing theory, as distinct from a stock pricing theory, as distinct from an option pricing theory. We recognize that it is a fundamental dissimilarity between, for example, debt and equity securities that while a company is contractually obligated to make interest payments, it is not similarly bound to pay dividends, which will normally be *contingent* upon a company remaining profitable. This, it is often said, is a crucial difference which accounts for the need to take a substantially different approach towards the valuation of a share of stock, relative to that taken towards the valuation of a bond.

The idea that this "crucial difference" makes stock valuation a qualitatively different kind of thing from bond valuation is, however, a pernicious myth, for it involves a confusion between *entitlements* and *receipts.* Consider: the interest to which a corporate bond confers entitlement is contingent upon the company's having the cash available to make the interest payments as and when they are due. The *obligation* of a company to make, for example, a bond interest payment must be differentiated from the payment *actually being made.* In assessing the true value of a security, our concern is with the payments we anticipate *actually receiving* from our investment, and not about entitlements *per se.* For the rational investor, all the promises in the world to make interest or dividend payments are worth nothing (or "less than the paper they're written on") if the promisor does not have the financial wherewithal to live up to his obligations.

A higher likelihood that payments will be made means a higher value ascribable to the promises to make such payments. This is why banks perform credit analyses on prospective borrowers (to assess the likelihood of being paid in full and on time) and why they charge lower interest rates to their more creditworthy customers (because here the likelihood of being paid in full and on time is high). An investor's rational assessment of the value of a financial security, in other words, entails answering two questions: (i) what amounts am I likely to receive from the investment, and (ii) how likely is it that I will receive them? The first of these questions relates to *reward*, the second to *risk*.

A satisfactory tool for analyzing the formal relationships between the risk associated with a security (that is, the contingency associated with the entitlements it confers) and that security's value was first evolved and developed by option pricing theorists in the early 1970s. The fact that it was in the context of options that such a tool was evolved is no doubt to be explained by the fact that receipts from options are more contingent than those from any other type of financial security.[1]

As the analysis of the formal features of the relationship between risk, reward and securities values progresses, some

---

[1] For those already possessing some familiarity with options, this point can be elaborated as follows. Compare, say, a call option on a share of XYZ Corporation stock to a share of the stock itself. Suppose the value of the XYZ share today is $25. Suppose, also, that there exists an option to buy one XYZ share at a price of $20. This option, let us say, is available at a cost of $5. If the option were purchased and exercised today it would yield no profit, for the option holder would be paying an aggregate of $25—$5 for the option and $20 for the exercise—in order to receive in return something with a market value of $25. But now suppose that the XYZ share rises in value to $30. This represents a 20% rise in the stock—no extraordinary event in today's volatile securities markets. Anyone who bought the share at $25 and now sells would realize a $5 profit, representing a 20% return on his original investment. The option holder would also clear a $5 profit if he were to exercise the option (cost: $5) for $20 and sell the share for $30. But his return is very substantially higher than 20%, for his initial investment was a mere $5. His return would, in fact, be a full 100% on his original investment. This neatly illustrates the high *leverage* of options: a push of just 20% on one end of the lever results here in a swing through 100% at the other end.

reasonably lengthy mathematical derivations are inevitably entailed. A key message of this book, however, is one of hope for the less mathematically-inclined. The highly technical forms of modern option pricing analyses have acted, no doubt, as impediments to a broad and general comprehension of the principles at work. But in themselves these principles are straightforward—every student of business and every person with an interest in understanding the principles from which much of our decision-making implicitly derives should be capable of grasping them. In Chapter 8, for example, we evolve a Do-It-Yourself option pricing model which reflects all the relationships between the variables making up an option's price in a way which presupposes no mathematical ability beyond a grasp of the most basic elements of arithmetic.

Chapter 2

2

The Time Value of Money and Discounted Cash Flow (DCF) Analysis

TIME VALUE

If you were lucky enough to win $10,000 in the state lottery, how would you feel? Elated, of course, but what if—when the time came to collect your prize money—you found that the $10,000 was to be paid in two installments, $5,000 today and $5,000 one year from now? You would almost certainly feel a little let-down, particularly if you had earmarked the money for a new car, or a once-in-a-lifetime world cruise. In order to enjoy the $10,000 car or holiday today, you would have to take the first $5,000 installment and borrow the balance. The borrowed $5,000 could then be repaid in one year, when the second installment of prize money arrives. The catch here, of course, is that along with your $5,000 loan repayment you would need to pay interest. If your bank charges 10% per annum, your $5,000 repayment—made one year down the road—would be accompanied by $500 of interest. This $500 represents one year's *time value* of $5,000 and is a function of whatever interest rates prevail. It is, you could say, the monetary opportunity that would derive from having the $5,000 working for you (earning interest, for example) for one year.

Money, in the form of cash, is a commodity. Money is also the principal yardstick against which we measure value (other, of course, than moral value). Monetary value can be assigned to all kinds of commodities, from pork bellies to Treasury bonds to gold. All those things whose value can be expressed in monetary terms also have time value.

Time value is one of the most fundamental concepts in finance. It plays a part in every business decision, from whether to buy this or that stock to settling on the terms of a major construction contract. The concept of time value implies no more than the idea that money—like any other asset—can be put to work for its owner and can, over time, earn the owner a return. In the case of cash, this return generally comes in the form of *interest.* The amount of interest associated with, for example, a bank deposit will be a function of the time over which the money is deposited and the interest rate paid by the bank. We term the amount of the deposit upon which the interest is computed and repayment made, its *principal amount.*

With bank deposits, the idea of interest and return is all very simple. Typically, we deposit, say, $100 with the bank at

8% p.a. and are paid $8 of interest each year, with $100 being returned to us at the end of the investment period. In such a case our original investment—$100—is equal to the principal amount of the deposit. The return earned on the amount of money we actually put up is 8% p.a., the same as the interest rate paid by the bank. Bonds, however, are liquid investments. A bond can be bought and re-sold, sometimes at a price which differs from its principal amount. A bond that pays interest at a rate of 10% p.a. and which has a principal amount of $1,000, but which is bought for just $800 will have an overall return which exceeds 10% p.a. After all, $100 of interest received in respect of an investment costing just $800 represents substantially more than 10% p.a. It in fact amounts to a hefty 12.5% p.a. On top of this, the investor will get a repayment of $1,000 for an original investment of just $800. This boosts his percentage return higher still.

BONDS

To avoid confusion between the rate used to calculate the interest paid (in case of bonds, termed the *coupon rate* or simply the *coupon*) and the actual return conferred by an investment, we term the latter the *yield* of the investment. Suppose an investor with $800 to invest today for a period of one year is faced with the choice between (i) making a deposit at a major bank, which is paying interest at 8% p.a., and (ii) buying a bond with one year of life remaining. The bond, whose market price is $800, has a principal amount of $1,000 but pays a coupon of just 1% p.a. Compare the payoff of the deposit one year hence to that of the bond (see Figure 2–1).

Buying the bond for $800 will earn the investor a full $146 more than placing the $800 on deposit at the bank, despite the fact that the interest rate associated with the deposit is a full 7% p.a. higher than that associated with the bond.

Figure 2–1

	Deposit	Bond
Principal repayment	$800	$1,000
Plus one year's interest	$64	$10
	$864	$1,010

The total bank deposit payoff of $864 one year hence represents the amount obtained by *compounding* $800 over one year at a rate of 8% p.a. The $864 is termed the *future value* (FV) of $800, "compounded at 8% p.a. for one year" (the 8% p.a. in this context is sometimes referred to as the *compounding rate*). Conversely, we often describe the $800 original investment as the *present value* (PV) or *net present value* of $864. It is the amount obtained by *discounting* $864 over one year at a *discount rate* of 8% p.a.

The payoff from the bond, meanwhile, is $1,010 from an original investment of $800. This represents a yield of a full 26.25% p.a. This yield is the interest rate that we would need to earn on a conventional bank deposit in order to arrive at the same future value after one year of $1,010.

Returning to the bank deposit, suppose $800 was deposited for two years at 8% p.a.; what then would be the investor's total payoff at the deposit's maturity (i.e., the deposit's future value, or FV)? At the end of the first year, the original investment will have been compounded to a total of $864 of principal and interest. This is automatically deemed reinvested and is the amount on which interest will be earned for the second year. After one year, then, we have $800 × (1+8%), (i.e., $864), and after two years we have an aggregate of $800 × (1+8%) × (1+8%)—i.e., $933.12. After n years we would have $800 × $(1+8\%)^n$.

We have now derived a general equation for use in *Discounted Cash Flow* (DCF) *analysis*. This equation links (i) the original investment (the PV), (ii) the aggregate principal and interest payoff (FV), (iii) the yield of the investment (or, if working backward to find the PV, the discount rate), and (iv) the number of times the investment is deemed invested and reinvested (the number of *compounding periods*, in the above case the number of years). If the yield or discount rate is r% per compounding period and the number of compounding periods is n, then:

$$FV = PV \times (1+r)^n$$

Alternatively,

$$PV = \frac{FV}{(1+r)^n} \qquad 2(1)$$

Using this equation we can find the yield of the 1% bond purchased for $800:

$$\$800 = \frac{\$1{,}010}{(1+r)^1}$$

$$r = 26.25\% \text{ p.a.}$$

A CLOSER LOOK AT BONDS AND DISCOUNTED CASH FLOWS

A bond is a piece of paper that typically entitles the holder to receive cash payments of interest ("coupon payments") throughout its life, up to its maturity. At maturity the principal is repaid, along with the final installment of interest. The salient investment characteristics of a bond include:

- the credit standing of the issuer (the obligor);
- the coupon rate (which is multiplied by the principal amount of the bond to compute interest payable); and
- the maturity date, on which holders of the bonds receive repayment of principal.[1]

Dealers refer to bonds by these characteristics. A typical reference might be to the, "International Widget eight-and-a-halves of July '94," meaning that the bonds represent obligations of International Widget (the issuer), that they have a coupon of 8½ % p.a., and that principal is due to be repaid in July, 1994.

Suppose that these International Widget bonds pay interest once each year ("annually") on July 15th, and are repaid in one lump sum (have a bullet maturity) on July 15th, 1994. An investor who, on July 15th, 1990, purchases $1,000 principal amount of the bonds will be due to receive the interest payments and principal repayment scheduled in Figure 2–2, assuming he holds the bonds to their maturity. Now, if we know that he bought those bonds at a price which afforded him a yield of 9.5% p.a., we can determine the dollar price. In order to do this we simply present value each of the future cash flows associated with the bond using Equation 2(1). The discount rate used will be the yield of 9.5% p.a. Since the bond represents the investor's entitlement to each of the future

[1] Some bonds provide for repayment of principal in installments. These are said to "amortize" over the installments period. A bond which repays principal in one lump sum is said to have a "bullet" maturity.

Figure 2–2

Date	Cash Flow	PV of Cash Flow	
July 15, 1991	$85	$35/1.095^1 =$	$77.63
July 15, 1992	$85	$85/1.095^2 =$	$70.89
July 15, 1993	$85	$85/1.095^3 =$	$64.74
July 15, 1994	$1,085	$1,085/1.095^4 =$	$754.70
Aggregate of PVs of cash flows (i.e., bond price)			$967.96

cash flows, the aggregate of the present values of each of those cash flows represents the value of the bond itself.

Using this characterization—bond price = aggregate of the PVs of the bond's cash flows—we can derive an equation linking (i) the bond price with (ii) the discount rate, (iii) the maturity, and (iv) the bond's cash flows:

$$\textit{Bond price} = \sum_{j=1}^{n} \frac{CF_j}{(1+r)^j} \qquad 2(2)$$

where:

n is the maturity of the bond in compounding periods (years);

CF_j is the bond's cash flow in compounding period j; and

r is the discount rate expressed in % per compounding period.

If the interest rate environment and the credit standing of International Widget are such that the market demands a 9.5% p.a. yield from International Widget bonds, then we know that the 8½s of July '94 will be priced in the market at around 96.796% of their principal amount. If we know the price of the bonds is 96.796% of their principal amount then we can derive the yield of 9.5% p.a.

The yield of a bond is the *internal rate of return* (IRR) of the cash flows associated with the bond. While bonds have yields, sets of cash flows have IRRs. In the case of the International Widget bonds yielding 9.5% p.a., the first such cash flow is a negative cash flow (that is, a cash *outflow* from the point of view of the investor) of $967.96, and the subsequent cash flows are positive cash flows (inflows, or receipts) of $85 per year in each year up to (and including) 1993 and $1,085 in 1994.

The techniques of DCF analysis are relatively simple in themselves, as will become apparent with use, but they are complicated and made daunting by the somewhat confusing terminology that surrounds them and in which discussion of them is couched. Remember, the variables of DCF analysis are

- yield, or discount rate, or internal rate of return;
- coupon, or interest rate;
- life of the investment, or maturity;
- future value, or principal repayment; and

- present value, or market price.

Knowing any four of the above, we can determine the fifth.

COMPOUNDING PERIODS

Before leaving this preliminary review of DCF analysis, there is one element that requires some elaboration, for it is often a source of confusion and irritation to the emerging analyst. This element is the frequency with which an investment is compounded, and it has important implications for the yield of an investment, or the IRR of a set of cash flows.

Yields, discount rates, internal rates of return, coupons and interest rates are all typically expressed in terms of "percent per annum." Not all such yields and rates are, however, directly comparable. This will be clear to anyone who has reflected on the way in which banks and finance companies sometimes advertise one interest rate and then take pains to point out, for example, that the "annual percentage rate equivalent" of this rate is such-and-such. If the interest rate expressed in percent per annum is not the annual percentage rate, what is it?

The disparity lies with the frequency of compounding. Go back to our earlier analysis of a two year bank deposit which afforded interest of 8% p.a. At the end of the first year the original investment, along with the first year's interest, was deemed reinvested. In the second year of the deposit, nominally more interest was earned than in the first year, because interest was accrued on not only our original investment but also on the first year's interest. The deposit, by virtue of being deemed reinvested each year, is said to accrue, or to *compound,* annually.

Now consider what would have happened had the deposit had been compounded every half year, or *semi-annually.* At the end of half a year we would have accrued half a year's interest at a rate of 8% p.a.—i.e., interest equal to 4% of our original investment. This would now have been deemed reinvested for the second half year period, again at a rate of 8% p.a. For the second half of the year, we would now be earning interest on not only our original investment, but also on one-half year's worth of interest on that original investment. For every \$100 of our original investment we earn \$4 of interest during the first half year and 4% × \$104 during the second half-year. At the end of the first full year, we have \$108.16 to be deemed reinvested, rather than the \$108 we would have received had our investment been compounded annually. The more frequently our investment is compounded, the better off we are because the more we benefit from earning interest on interest. We would, using our deposit example, need to earn 8.16% p.a. in interest on an annually compounded deposit to be as well off as the individual whose deposit earns 8% p.a., compounded semi-annually. Our 8.16% p.a. is said to be the *"annually compounded equivalent"* (or simply the "annual equivalent") of 8% p.a. compounded semi-annually.

In valuing the International Widget 8½s of July '94, we noted that the bonds paid interest annually. In computing the bond's yield at the price of 96.796% we calculated the present value of each cash flow assuming annual compounding periods. That is, for the cash flow CF_j (the jth cash flow received by the investor), j was expressed as an integral number of years. When dealing with coupons or interest rates, always know what frequency of interest payment you are using, and always take care to use this same frequency for the purpose of compounding, or discounting, to find future values, present values, yields, discount rates, or IRRs.

A simple example should serve to illustrate the point. Virtually all U.S. bonds—both Treasury and corporate bonds—pay interest semi-annually (each half year). Suppose this were the case with the International Widget 8½s of July '94. The cash flows associated with $1,000 principal amount of the bonds would then look somewhat different from those set out in Figure 2–2 (see Figure 2–3).

Being paid our first installment of interest after six months gives us the opportunity to re-invest and earn additional interest. Semi-annual payment of an 8½ % p.a. coupon is more valuable to an investor than annual payment because of this ability to earn additional interest on interest.

We can calculate the IRR of the semi-annual cash flows set out in Figure 2–3 using Equation 2(2), but we must make sure we conform the frequency of compounding to the frequency

Figure 2–3

Date	Cash Flow
January 15, 1991	$42.50
July 15, 1991	$42.50
January 15, 1992	$42.50
July 15, 1992	$42.50
January 15, 1993	$42.50
July 15, 1993	$42.50
January 15, 1994	$42.50
July 15, 1994	$1,042.50

of payment. The frequency of compounding is half-yearly, giving us eight rather than four compounding periods. Thus, in Equation 2(2), for '*n*' we must substitute '8'. Meanwhile, '*r*' represents the discount rate, or yield, of the bond *per compounding period*, in this case, per half year. When we solve Equation 2(2) for *r*, therefore, we will have derived a yield expressed in percent *per half year*. As earlier noted, yields, discount rates and IRRs are all generally expressed in terms of percent per annum. To make the adjustment from "percent per half year" to "percent per annum" we simply multiply by two—the number of half years in a year.

To repeat, it is key when dealing with yields, discount rates, IRRs, coupons and interest rates in DCF calculations to maintain consistent time units. For the purpose of applying Equation 2(2), if the bond in question pays interest semi-annually, express its yield (the discount rate) as a semi-annually compounded yield and its maturity in half years, whatever the variable for which you may be solving.

If the subtleties of semi-annual versus annual compounding are not yet absolutely clear, don't worry. Talk of "annual coupons, semi-annually compounded" or "semi-annual coupons, annually compounded" is confusing to everybody at first. Try always to think of and to express yields, discount rates and IRRs in terms of percent per compounding period. Do this and confusion soon will be a thing of the past.

We will now leave discussion of compounding periods. Henceforth, all yields, discount rates and IRRs will be assumed annually compounded and it shall be assumed, in defiance of U.S. bond market convention, that unless otherwise specified, all bonds confer annual coupon payments.

Chapter 3

3

An Introduction to Forward Pricing and the Arbitrage Pricing Method

FORWARD AND FUTURES CONTRACTS

A *forward contract* is one by which one of the contracting parties (the seller) agrees to sell a particular thing—the *underlying commodity*—to the other (the buyer) at a particular point in the future. The contract will specify the price to be paid by the buyer (the *forward price*), along with the date (the forward or *delivery* date) on which delivery of, and payment for, the underlying commodity is to take place. Thus, if you own a one-year BMW 325i forward contract, you have entered into an agreement to take delivery of the car one year hence at a pre-determined price.

Forward contracts are neither standardized nor exchange-traded. They are contracts struck between particular parties to suit their own needs. As a result of being fashioned to suit particular needs, they are in many cases highly illiquid, since what suits one party's requirements often will not suit another's. However, if the rights and obligations under forward contracts *are* assigned or traded, there will normally be an up-front payment made. This payment might be made either by the assignor (i.e., the seller of the contract) to the assignee (the buyer), or vice versa.

For the most part, forward contracts are struck between producers and consumers of the underlying commodity. These parties will be brought together by commodity traders. However, a great deal of the activity which takes place between banks in the foreign exchange markets involves buying and selling currencies for forward delivery pursuant to forward contracts.

Futures contracts are in many respects similar to forward contracts. They provide for forward payment (of what in the futures market is generally termed the *futures price*, rather than the *forward price*) and delivery of a wide variety of underlying commodities, including stocks, stock indexes, agricultural and mineral commodities, interest rates and currencies. In contrast to forward contracts, however, futures contracts are traded on major stock and futures exchanges. To facilitate such trading, the contracts are highly *standardized*. Delivery dates fall on a specified day of each month, the quality of the underlying commodity is standardized, delivery location and settlement procedures are standardized, and so on. This standardization facilitates *liquidity* in the contract since traders know exactly what they are getting when they make a trade. They also know exactly what the risk of non-performance by their counterparty happens to be, since futures contracts are typically guaranteed by the clearing house of the exchange on which they are traded.

Because of their liquidity and the ease of executing an offsetting position (buying a contract to offset an identical contract sold, for example), actual delivery of the underlying commodity rarely occurs with futures contracts. Futures contracts tend to be used to offset economic risks, rather than as a means of securing a supply of the underlying commodity—another respect in which they differ from forward contracts.

Despite their differences, the principles governing the economic analysis of forward contracts and futures contracts are identical. So, for the purposes of the examples of this chapter, we will concentrate on forward contracts and will use the expression "forward price" in preference to the perhaps less suggestive "futures price," which is exactly analogous.

THE FORWARD PRICE

Many people use forward and futures contracts to *hedge* their costs. For example, suppose an oil consumer fears a rise in the price of crude over the coming year and thus wishes to lock-in his cost of crude for use in one year's time. He might, in such circumstances, do one of two things. First, he might simply buy the crude today and store it for a year. Second, he might buy oil forward, giving him what we term a *long* forward position in oil. This means entering into a forward contract with, say, an oil producer (who might hold different expectations for the oil market) pursuant to which the consumer undertakes to take delivery of—and to pay for—a specified number of barrels on the one year delivery date. But now the question arises, what is the appropriate forward price?

Suppose that the *spot* or *cash* price—the price for immediate payment and delivery—of Light Sweet Crude (LSC) oil is $26 per barrel. If the oil consumer wants to lock-in a one-year price for, say, 1,000 barrels, the spot purchase strategy will cost him $26,000. On the other hand, if the forward price per barrel is *f*, the forward contract strategy will require him to make payment of the aggregate forward price (1,000 × *f*) one year hence. Look closely at the timing of these cash flows, as set out in Figure 3–1.

The spot purchase and storage of crude (Alternative 1 in Figure 3–1) entails an initial outlay which is $26,000 higher than that entailed by the forward contract strategy. With $26,000 at his disposal the oil consumer might either buy the crude in the spot market or, alternatively, enter into the forward contract and then deposit the $26,000 into his bank. Suppose his bank's one-year deposit rate is 8% p.a. The $26,000 one-year deposit then would be repaid in an amount of $28,080 (the principal repayment of $26,000 plus interest of $2,080). It would be repaid at exactly the time when the oil consumer is required to pay the forward price and take delivery of the 1,000 barrels of crude. Now suppose the

Figure 3–1

	Alternative 1	Alternative 2
Time	**Spot Purchase**	**Forward Purchase**
Today	Pay $26,000	Pay nothing
1 year hence	Pay nothing	Pay 1,000 × *f*

forward price, *f*, is \$27 per barrel. Only \$27,000 of the maturing deposit plus interest would then be needed to pay for crude under the forward contract. The additional \$1,080 would go back into the oil consumer's pocket. By buying the oil forward the consumer would, in other words, be \$1,080 better off than if he were to opt to buy 1,000 barrels in the spot market and store crude for a year.

The important thing to bear in mind about this example is that, so far as the oil consumer's interest in crude is concerned, the alternative strategies of, on the one hand, entering into the one year LSC forward contract plus making the one year bank deposit and, on the other hand, making the spot purchase and subsequently storing the 1,000 barrels of LSC are equally viable. We might (and henceforth will) say that a portfolio comprising the forward contract plus the deposit *replicates* a portfolio comprising the stored oil. But while the two alternatives are identical from the point of view of giving access to the requisite number of barrels of oil one year hence, their cost is very different. Both entail an up-front outlay of \$26,000, but one leaves the oil consumer with a surplus of \$1,080 one year hence.

Where two portfolios effectively replicate each other but are priced differently then, assuming we have active and liquid markets, the entrepreneur is presented with a profit opportunity. He will buy the cheap portfolio and sell the replicating (but more expensive) portfolio, in what is termed an *arbitrage* transaction. Buying the underpriced portfolio alone, of course, is not sufficient to guarantee a profit, for this would leave the entrepreneur exposed to a potential loss if the price of the underlying commodity shifted in the wrong direction (suppose, for example, he could only unload the oil when he takes delivery at the then prevailing price of \$20 per barrel). The sale of the replicating portfolio is said to *hedge* this exposure.

In the case of the oil futures contract, the opportunity to profit from an arbitrage transaction would be eliminated only if the forward price under the forward contract is $28.08 per barrel, for the aggregate forward price only then would equal the $28,080 from the maturing deposit. This would be the appropriate or *break-even* forward price—fair to both producer and consumer—to set in connection with the LSC forward contract. The break-even forward price is a function of the spot price of the underlying commodity, the length of time to the delivery date and interest rates.

THE CONTRACT VALUE

Sometimes we do not have any say in the fixing of the forward price in connection with a particular forward contract. This will be the case, for example, when we acquire the rights and obligations under a contract from someone else—someone who had entered into the contract at some time in the past and who now wishes to assign it. In such cases the contract will generally have a value associated with it. If the actual forward price associated with a particular contract is below the break-even forward price, then the contract will have a positive value to its owner: it commits him to pay a lower price for the underlying commodity than the alternative spot purchase and storage strategy.

For example, suppose you are a (very modest) oil consumer and wish to acquire a contract requiring you to buy just one barrel of LSC for payment and delivery one year hence (we generally say, "for one year delivery"). A contract is on offer which carries a forward price of just $19 per barrel. The spot price of Light Sweet Crude is, as in the above example, $26 per barrel and the one year deposit rate is again 8% p.a. The $19 forward price is substantially below the $28.08 break-even forward price of the crude, and this will be reflected in the market value of the contract, which we will call *c*. In this case, *c* will be around $9.08. It will not be *exactly* $9.08 since this amount represents the difference between the break-even and the actual *forward* price of LSC. The market value of the forward contract *today* will thus reflect a present value adjustment to the $9.08.

When analyzing forward contracts and futures strategies in order to determine either the break-even forward price or the value of a particular contract, it is invariably illuminating to tabulate the cash flows associated with the contract and to compare them to the spot purchase alternative. These alternative cash flows as they apply to the example of the LSC

Figure 3–2

	Alternative 1	**Alternative 2**
Time	**Spot Purchase**	**Forward Purchase**
Today	Pay $26; store one barrel for 1 year	Pay *c* for forward contract; deposit $26-*c* for 1 year at 8% p.a.
1 year hence	Take delivery from storage of one barrel	Receive ($26–*c*) × $(1.08)^1$ of interest plus principal; pay $19 forward price; take delivery of one barrel

forward contract with a $19 per barrel forward price are set out in Figure 3–2.

When we talk about forward pricing or the valuation of futures contracts, we are talking about the precise relationship between the value of the rights and obligations conferred by a forward or futures contract and, among other things, the forward price, the spot price of the underlying commodity, and the delivery date. Understanding this relationship is, of course, bread-and-butter to those who trade forward and futures contracts—that is, to those who acquire and assign the rights and obligations under the contracts in the interbank markets and on the major futures markets of Chicago and New York. The above examples should be sufficient to persuade you that the key to forward and futures pricing and valuation is—once again—time value.

MAKING A MILLION DOLLARS: THE GREAT BMW ARBITRAGE STRATEGY

Suppose a close friend of yours—owner of a major BMW dealership—is experiencing such demand for what he euphemistically terms "pre-owned" 300-series cars that he wishes to commit to pay you $1,000 today for each one-year old 300-series car with which you agree to supply him in one year's time. He will commit to pay you $20,000 per car upon the one-year delivery date. In other words, your friend wishes to buy BMWs forward, for one-year delivery. His forward price is $20,000 per car and his up-front price—the value, *c*, which he ascribes to the forward contract—is $1,000 per underlying car. He will take as many of the cars as you can contract to sell on these terms.

Now suppose that the cost of renting a new BMW 325i model for one year is $11,000, payable up-front. A portfolio which replicates the one-year rental contract can be constructed using a forward contract, the spot purchase of a car, and a suitable borrowing strategy. Consider:

The Rental Contract

Entering into the rental contract entails paying $11,000 today, taking delivery of the car, and returning a one-year old BMW 325i to the rental company one year hence. The net effect of the transaction, in other words, is to confer use of the car for one year for an up-front outlay of $11,000.

The Replicating Portfolio

Suppose that the spot price of each 325i is $28,000. Now suppose that you buy one car, for which you put up $11,000 in cash. You finance a further $16,000 of the car's $28,000 purchase price with a one-year loan and the remaining $1,000 by selling a one-year forward contract on the car to your dealer friend. The cash effect of these transactions is a net up-front outlay of $11,000. But you also enjoy use for one year of the car which you purchased for $28,000. At the end of the year it has to be delivered under the terms of the forward contract.

To this extent the replicating portfolio comprising the spot purchase of the car, the $16,000 borrowing and the sale of the forward contract is identical to the rental contract. But is its cost identical? That is, what happens when you come to repay your $16,000 borrowing—can you do so from the receipt of the $20,000 forward price?

The answer, clearly, is that it all depends upon the prevailing level of interest rates. If the one-year borrowing rate is 10% p.a. we can show that there exists an arbitrage opportunity, and that it can be exploited to earn a million dollars. This is how it would work:

(1) You buy 417 BMW 325is in the spot market for the spot price of $28,000 per car. Total outlay: $11,676,000.

(2) You rent out the 417 cars at the one-year rental rate of $11,000 per car. Total received: $4,587,000.

(3) You sell 417 cars for one year delivery at a forward price of $20,000 per car. The purchaser of the cars forward—the dealer—makes you an up-front payment of $1,000 per car. Total received up-front: $417,000.

(4) You borrow the $6,672,000 remaining of the purchase price from your bank, using a one-year loan at 10% p.a.

Together, these transactions result in a net outlay today of zero and the simultaneous receipt and re-delivery of the 417 cars. In other words, the up-front cash-in and cash-out cancel themselves and cars-in and cars-out cancel themselves. All you do now is sit and wait for one year to elapse. At the end of the year, you do the following:

(5) You receive the 417 returned rental cars, pursuant to (2) above.

(6) You deliver the 417 one-year-old cars to your dealer friend pursuant to the forward contract under (3) above. In return you receive the aggregate $8,340,000 (i.e. 417 × $20,000) forward price.

(7) You repay your bank loan pursuant to (4) above, the principal and interest on which aggregates \$7,339,200 (i.e., \$6,672,000 plus one year of interest at 10% p.a.).

Together, these transactions mean (i) the receipt and simultaneous re-delivery of the 417 cars, (ii) the receipt of \$8,340,000 by way of the forward price, and (iii) the payment of \$7,339,200 by way of principal and interest in respect of your loan. In other words, you have \$1,000,800 to pocket! Without exposing yourself to any net cash outlay or to any risk at all—excepting the risk of default on the part of the various other parties involved—you have made a profit exceeding one million dollars.

Again, the important thing to note in connection with this example is that the profit potential—the arbitrage—arises by virtue of a price disparity between one portfolio and a replicating portfolio. Transactions (2) and (5) above together represent no more than the sale of 417 rental contracts, while transactions (1), (3), (4), (6) and (7) together represent the purchase of 417 of the replicating portfolios.

What if the interest rate on one-year borrowings was, say, 35% p.a., rather than 10% p.a.? Your original \$6,672,000 bank borrowing would then be repaid with principal and interest aggregating \$9,007,200. When it came time to repay the bank loan with the proceeds from the forward contract you would find yourself \$667,200 short—there would be a distressing loss on the transaction. In a 35% interest-rate environment you would find that only if the forward price were \$21,600 per car, so that you received a total of \$9,007,200 by way of the forward price, would the transaction represent a break-even proposition and no arbitrage profit opportunity exist.

We can, in fact, always calculate the no-arbitrage forward price for any commodity as a function of its spot price, the delivery date, interest rates and 'rental' costs. In the case of the BMWs in a 35% p.a. borrowing rate environment, when the forward contract costs $1,000 per car then the break-even forward price, at which no profit or loss is possible, is $21,600 per car. If the market is quoting $1,000 for a contract with a forward price which is *higher* than $21,600, then you—as an entrepreneur—should sell the replicating portfolio (which contains the overpriced forward contract) and hedge your exposure to the possibility of loss due to a change in the price of BMWs by buying the rental contracts. Conversely, if the market is quoting $1,000 for a contract with a lower forward price, you should look at the economics of buying the replicating portfolio and selling the rental contracts in a strategy identical to the seven-step transaction outlined above.

DERIVING A GENERAL EQUATION FOR FORWARD PRICING

In order to derive a general equation for the pricing of forward and futures contracts, let's recap the methodology used to determine the forward price of BMWs at which the arbitrage potential is eliminated.

First, look at a BMW 325i rental contract and consider how to replicate its purchase with a portfolio comprising a spot purchase, a forward position and a bank loan. In the break-even situation, in which no arbitrage opportunity exists, the cash inflows and outflows associated with the *sale* of the rental contract will be canceled-out by those associated with the *purchase* of the replicating portfolio. We can tabulate the cash flows associated with the sale of one rental contract and the purchase of one replicating portfolio, as in Figure 3–3.

Figure 3–3

		Buy Replicating Portfolio			
Time	**Sell Contract**	**Buy Car Spot**	**Sell Futures Contract**	**Loan**	**Net**
Today	$11,000	<$28,000>	$1,000	$16,000	$0
One year hence	N/A	N/A	$21,6000	<$21,6000>	$0

Note that we follow convention by enclosing *negative* cash flows—cash *out*flows—in brackets.

While in the BMW arbitrage example a single up-front rental payment was assumed, rental contracts more often provide for periodic rental payments to be made. Hence, in deriving a general equation, it will do to keep the possibility of a series of rental installments in mind and denote the aggregate present value of all rental payments by '*PV(R)*'. Payments in respect of spot purchases are, by definition, made up-front.[1] Let us denote the cash *flow* (singular) associated with the spot purchase by '*S*'. The cash flows associated with the forward contract, meanwhile, can be broken down into two component parts, the up-front price paid by the buyer of the contract—call it *c*—and the forward price, also paid by the buyer—call it *f*.

The cash flows associated with the loan can similarly be broken down into two components—the amount borrowed and the amount repaid. The amount borrowed from the bank is to cover the shortfall between the amount received from the sale of the rental contract (*PV(R)*) plus the amount received from sale of the forward contract (*c*) on the one hand and the spot price paid for the car (*S*) on the other. In other words, the amount to be borrowed will be *S–(PV(R)+c),* or *S–PV(R)–c.* The repayment will comprise the lump-sum of principal and interest due to the bank on the delivery date. The repayment is simply the future value of *S–PV(R)–c,* compounded at the appropriate rate. From the equation for present values (Equation 2(1)) derived in Chapter 2 we know that the future value of an amount is that amount multiplied by $(1+r)^n$, where *r* is the compounding rate expressed in percent per compounding period and *n* is the number of compounding periods.

---

[1] Although, of course, they may be financed by, for example, a loan from the seller in the form of some sort of installment plan. But payment in installments really represents two component transactions: a seller's loan and a true spot purchase.

Now we are in a position to link all these elements. We know that all the up-front cash flows cancel out (see Figure 3–3)—that is, that the rental contract price received, less the spot price paid for the commodity, plus the forward contract price received, plus the amount of the loan received from the bank, equals zero. But, less trivially, we also know that in the no-arbitrage situation all the future cash flows cancel out—that is, that the forward price received, less the principal and interest repaid to the bank, equals zero:

$$f - (1+r)^n \times (S - PV(R) - c) = 0$$

Re-arranging to solve for the forward price, *f*, we have:

$$f = (1+r)^n \times (S - PV(R) - c) \qquad 3(1)$$

This is the general equation for forward and futures pricing. It can be re-arranged to solve for *c*:

$$c = S - PV(R) - \frac{f}{(1+r)^n}$$

Note that $f/(1+r)^n$ represents the present value of the futures price, call it *PV(f)*, discounted at *r*% per discounting period (see Equation 2(1)). Hence:

$$c = S - PV(R) - PV(f)$$

or:

$$S = c + PV(R) + PV(f) \qquad 3(1a)$$

This statement of Equation 3(1) has the merit of highlighting that in the no-arbitrage situation there will be equality between the cost of a spot purchase (*S*) on the one hand and, on the other, the cost of a replicating portfolio comprising a forward contract (cost: c), a rental contract (cost: $PV(R)$), and a deposit which matures in an amount equal to the forward price (deposit amount: $PV(f)$).

We can apply Equation 3(1) to determine the break-even BMW 325i forward price in a 10% p.a. interest rate environment:

S = \$28,000;

$PV(R)$ = \$11,000 (the rental cost being all payable up-front, and thus no discounting being required);

c = \$1,000;

r = 10% p.a.; and

n = 1 (i.e., one compounding period of one year).

Hence, from Equation 3(1):

$$f = (1+0.10)^1 \times (\$28{,}000 - \$11{,}000 - \$1{,}000)$$

$$= \$17{,}600$$

In other words, the break-even forward price is \$17,600, and had the dealer offered to buy, or indeed, to sell forward contracts bearing this forward price, then no arbitrage opportunity would exist to be exploited by any entrepreneur. In the 35% p.a. interest rate environment:

$$f = (1+0.35)^1 \times (\$16{,}000)$$

$$= \$21{,}600$$

Chapter 4

4

Pricing a Stock Future

STOCKS AND REPLICATES

Suppose you have $100 to invest in the stock of International Widget Corporation, which is currently trading at $100 per share. The prospective yield on the stock (which simply refers to the anticipated dividend for the year divided by the current stock price) is 5%. You believe, in other words, that (barring a catastrophic loss, of which you believe there is a negligible chance) Widget will pay a $5 per share dividend for the year. Suppose this dividend is to be paid in one lump sum one year hence. The cash flows associated with the purchase of one share of the company will then be as set out in Figure 4–1.

Figure 4–1

Time	Cash Flow
0 (i.e., today)	<$100>
One year hence	$5 [viz, the dividend] Note that at this point you also hold 1 share, which you could choose to sell for its current market value of, say, S_1

Now suppose that there is traded on a major exchange a one-year futures contract with a futures price (exactly analogous to a forward price) of $105.20 per Widget share. Our object is to determine the 'correct' or no-arbitrage price at which this contract should trade. We can, of course, use Equation 3(1) as just derived to do this. To drive home the methodology behind the derivation, however, it is as well to undertake the valuation of the Widget futures contract from first principles.

Our starting point is with the question, how can we use the futures contract to replicate the spot purchase of a Widget share? As in the case of BMWs, this replication can be achieved by (i) purchasing the one-year futures position in one Widget share, (ii) 'renting' the stock for one year, and (iii) borrowing or lending in appropriate amounts.

Constructing the Replicating Portfolio

The first component in the replicating portfolio is the futures contract. Third is the borrowing or lending component. If interest rates on one year deposits with the very highest quality banks are 10% p.a., then the \$105.20 futures price, expressed in terms of today's dollars (i.e., *PV(f)*) is \$105.20/1.1, or \$95.64. Thus, if you deposit \$95.64 today with a bank of the very highest quality, you will be repaid principal and interest aggregating \$105.20 one year hence. You will then be able to apply this amount to fulfilling your obligation to purchase one share under the futures contract. Depositing \$95.64 for one year[1] will thus be a part of the borrowing or lending component of the replicating portfolio.

Now let us look at the second component of the replicating portfolio—the 'renting' of the Widget share of stock. A spot purchase of a share of stock gives the purchaser the right to all the entitlements associated with the stock from day one. Ownership of a one-year futures contract, meanwhile, gives the owner the right to the entitlements associated with the stock only after he has paid the futures price and taken delivery of the stock one year hence. 'Renting' the stock consists of acquiring the entitlements associated with the stock during that one year, so as to complete the replicating portfolio.

Voting rights (the entitlement to vote in company meetings), entitlement to dividends, and entitlement to amounts in liquidation are the exhaustive entitlements conferred by stocks. Let us assume for the moment that Widget voting

[1] Note that you will be well advised to make this deposit only with a bank of the very highest quality, since your obligation to come up with the \$105.20 futures price one year hence is unconditional—there is no room to run the risk of having the bank fail if you wish to replicate not only the rewards but also the risks associated with a Widget share.

rights in themselves are of no economic value (perhaps because the company is as well run for the benefit of shareholders as it is capable of being). Additionally, we will assume that it is inconceivable that Widget will be liquidated during the coming year, and hence that entitlements to amounts in liquidation are of no relevance. Acquiring the entitlements associated with a share of Widget stock during the coming year—which is what renting a share for one year amounts to—thus rests only in the $5 of dividends accruing on the stock over the year. The PV of the dividend is thus the appropriate rental cost. It is simply the amount you would need to deposit today in order that you would be repaid principal and interest in the same amount and at the same time as dividends would be received from the stock. Making such a deposit is thus the final component of the borrowing or lending strategy associated with the replicating portfolio. Given that the Widget dividend amounts to $5 one year hence, the amount to be deposited at 10% p.a. is (by Equation 2(1)) $5/1.1, or $4.55.

Now we are in a position to tabulate the cash flows associated with our replicating portfolio, in order to determine the

Figure 4–2

Time	**Buy Shares Spot**	**Buy Futures Contract**	**Make Deposit of $95.64 plus $4.55**
Today	<$100>	<*c*>	<$95.64> + <$4.55>
One year hence	$5 + *S*	<$105.20> +*S*	$105.20 + $5

no-arbitrage price of a one-year futures contract on one underlying share with a futures price of \$105.20. This no-arbitrage price will be the futures price at which the cash flows associated with the Widget stock, as set out in Figure 4–1, exactly match those associated with the replicating portfolio.

We can now simply solve for *c*:

$$\$100 = \langle c \rangle + \langle \$95.64 \rangle + \langle \$4.55 \rangle$$

(Recall that angular brackets represent negative cash flows—cash outflows.) Hence

$$c = - \$0.19$$

As mentioned above, we might simply have used Equation 3(1) or, easier still, Equation 3(1a) to arrive at the same result:

$$S = c + PV(R) + PV(f)$$

Previously, we calculated $PV(f)$ to be \$95.64. S, meanwhile, is the \$100 spot price of the share, and $PV(R)$ is the rental cost of the share as we calculated it above—i.e., \$4.55. Hence:

$$c = \$100 - \$4.55 - \$95.64$$

$$= - \$0.19$$

Given, therefore, the current price of the Widget share, a 10% p.a. interest rate environment, and a \$5 expected dividend, we have calculated that the no-arbitrage value of a one year futures contract with a \$105.20 futures price is -\$0.19. Anyone who wished to acquire (to buy) such a contract should thus expect not to pay for it, but rather to be compensated 19 cents for assuming the obligation to pay the \$105.20 which ownership of the contract confers.

A NOTE CONCERNING DISCOUNT RATES AND RISK

Previously (see footnote, page 45) we alluded to the need, as part of the replicating portfolio, to deposit the $95.64 only with a bank of the very highest quality. This is because the obligation of the owner of the futures contract to come up with the $105.20 futures price one year hence is unconditional. There is no room to run the risk of having the bank fail if you, as the futures contract owner, wish to replicate not only the rewards but also the risks associated with a Widget share. But could we afford to deposit the $4.55 (which will, when repaid, replicate the Widget dividend) with a slightly riskier bank in order to earn an interest rate which is higher than the 10% p.a. being paid by the best banks?

Interest rates, discount rates, and yields reflect risk. Highly risky corporate bonds yield more than Treasury bonds, reflecting the much higher probability of a default. Generally, the riskier the investment, the higher the rate required to compensate the investor for assuming that risk. In the case of International Widget, we have already pointed out that the $5 dividend is a safe bet. Nevertheless, there is always a chance, no matter how slim, that the company may suffer a catastrophic loss during the year and cut or even pass its dividend entirely. The discount rate used to derive *PV(R)* should reflect this risk and, since the risk exceeds zero, the discount rate should exceed the riskless rate. The riskless interest rate is measured by the yield of U.S. Treasury obligations, since Treasury bills, notes and bonds are the safest dollar fixed-income investments (although we assumed above that rates obtained on deposits with the highest quality banks were also riskless rates). The amount by which the discount rate used to compute *PV(R)* should exceed the riskless rate is a matter for later in this book. For the moment, the important thing to bear in mind is that in applying Equations 2(1), 2(2) and 3(1), it is necessary to match the riskiness reflected in the discount rate to the riskiness of the cash flow which is being discounted, or future-valued.

EXPANDING THE GENERAL EQUATION FOR FORWARD PRICING

In deriving the general equation for forward pricing in the foregoing chapter, we noted that *PV(R)* denoted the cost, in present value terms, of renting the underlying commodity for the period up to the delivery date. In the case of a share of stock, we have seen that the rental cost is approximately equal to the dividends accruing on the stock. When the delivery date is more than one year away, *PV(R)* will denote the present value of a series of yearly dividends. We can adapt Equation 3(1) to reflect this quite simply.

In Chapter 1 we discovered how to determine the aggregate PV of a series of cash flows, such as the annual coupon payments associated with a bond, by discounting each of those cash flows at a rate of r% p.a. Now that we have distinguished between *riskless* and *risky* discount rates, it is necessary to refine our analysis. From now on, we will use r to signify a riskless discount rate, yield or interest rate, and R to signify a risky rate, reflecting whatever degree of risk is appropriate in the context of our analysis.

The risky discount rate, R, is appropriate for the purpose of discounting a series of coupons (or anticipated dividends) accruing on anything other than a riskless investment. If we label the first year's coupon payment associated with any non-riskless bond CF_1, the second year's coupon CF_2 and so on, up to the nth year's cash flow of CF_n, then the aggregate PV of the cash flows CF_1 through CF_n is:

$$\frac{CF_1}{(1+R)^1} + \frac{CF_2}{(1+R)^2} \cdots\cdots + \frac{CF_{n-1}}{(1+R)^{n-1}} + \frac{CF_n}{(1+R)^n}$$

In other words:

$$PV(CF_1,....,CF_n) = \sum_{j=1}^{n} \frac{CF_j}{(1+R)^j}$$

We can now substitute this expression for $PV(CF_1,....,CF_n)$ for $PV(R)$ in our general equation for forward and futures pricing—Equation 3(1)—in order to deal effectively with long-dated forward and futures contracts (those where $n > 1$) on income-bearing commodities:

$$f = (1+r)^n \left(S - \sum_{j=1}^{n} \frac{CF_j}{(1+R)^j} - c \right) \qquad 4(1)$$

This is the expanded general forward and futures pricing equation, in which

f is the forward or futures price associated with a given contract;

r is the riskless interest or discount rate per compounding period;

n is the number of compounding periods up to the delivery date;

S is the spot price of the underlying commodity;

CF_j is the cash flow associated with the underlying commodity in the jth compounding period;

R is the risky interest or discount rate per compounding period, by which it is appropriate to present value the cash flows associated with the underlying commodity; and

c is the no-arbitrage price of the futures contract in question.

SUMMARY

The no-arbitrage value of a forward or futures contract on a particular underlying commodity—be it a BMW or a share of stock—is a function of

- the forward or futures price associated with the contract;
- the spot price of the underlying commodity;
- the length of time up until the delivery date;
- the 'rental' cost of the underlying commodity, as represented by the income accruing on the commodity during the period up to the delivery date; and
- interest or discount rates for this period.

It was concluded that in order to eliminate a potential for guaranteed profit the cost—expressed in PV terms—of the replicating portfolio comprising a forward or futures contract plus a 'rental' contract, along with the appropriate borrowing or lending strategy, must equal the spot price of the underlying commodity. Hence the general equation for forward and futures pricing (Equation 3(1)).

In applying the general equation in its Equation 3(1a) form, we need to use two different discount rates, one a riskless rate for the purpose of computing *PV(f)*, and the other a rate which reflects the risk associated with the income accruing on the underlying commodity, for the purpose of computing *PV(R)*. The theoretical basis for determining the proper and appropriate relationship between riskless and risky interest and discount rates is fascinating, but it is a topic for later chapters.

In addition to the matter of the risk reflected in the interest or discount rates, there is the question whether these should be deposit rates (i.e. the rates available to those who *lend* to banks) or borrowing rates. Borrowing rates are, obviously, generally higher than deposit rates.

If the forward contract is expensive relative to the spot price of the underlying commodity, then the arbitrageur will *buy* the commodity in the spot market and hedge by *selling* the replicating portfolio. Selling the replicating portfolio will comprise (i) selling the forward contract, (ii) *borrowing* an amount equal to *PV(f)* (for the purpose of computing that amount he will, of course, use a borrowing rate), and (iii) renting out the commodity. In this case, since the rental payment is to be received, use a deposit or lending rate to compute *PV(R)*.

If the forward contract looks cheap relative to the spot market, the arbitrageur will assess his profit potential by planning to undertake the above transactions the other way round, with the commodity being *sold* spot and the replicating portfolio being *purchased* as a hedge. In this case, he will use a deposit (lending) rate in computing *PV(f)* and a borrowing rate in computing *PV(R)*. The important thing, however, is neither to memorize the appropriate rate to use in a given situation, nor to memorize the general equation for forward and futures pricing itself. Rather, it is for all students to understand the logic of the forward and futures pricing methodology.

Our method of designing a replicating portfolio comprising a forward position plus rental and equating the cost of this replicating portfolio to the spot price of the underlying commodity serves to find the forward or futures price at which a riskless profit opportunity is eliminated. The strategy described for profiting from the over-pricing of BMW futures, for example, was riskless, not in the sense that the various parties involved (the forward buyer, banks and so on) could not default on their obligations, but in the sense that the profitability of the strategy did not depend upon our guessing correctly what the market for one-year-old BMWs would be one year down the road. In using the strategy we lock-in our profit today and are immune from the effects of changing markets. Interest and discount rates, the spot price and rental costs in effect today all combine to dictate a break-even or 'correct' one year forward price for any commodity or, given a forward or futures price, the value of the relevant contract. Any deviation from this price may present profit opportunities.

The strategy by which an entrepreneur exploits opportunities deriving from mispricing or pricing deviations is termed an "arbitrage strategy." It entails buying a commodity in one market and simultaneously locking-in a profit by selling something with substantially the same price behavior in another, in such a way that one is not exposed to a risk of loss in the event of price changes. In the BMW case, the entrepreneur—we can call him an "arbitrageur"—was buying cars in the spot market (for payment and delivery today) and simultaneously selling the replicating portfolio.

The above approach adopted to calculate correct, no-arbitrage forward prices is termed "the arbitrage pricing method" or simply "arbitrage pricing," and it is the foundation not only of forward and futures pricing but—as we shall see—also of modern option pricing models.

For the sake of driving the arbitrage pricing method home, the following chapter is devoted to the application of arbitrage pricing to the pricing or valuation of other common financial instruments, including forward foreign exchange rates and bond futures.

Chapter 5

5

Further Excursions in Forward and Futures Pricing

THE DETERMINATION OF FORWARD FOREIGN EXCHANGE RATES

Exchange rates represent the value of one currency expressed in terms of another—the amount of currency A that can be bought for one unit of currency B. As with BMWs and stocks, the 'correct' price or value of a foreign currency for forward or future payment and delivery (the correct *forward foreign exchange rate*) is determined by the spot price of the foreign currency (the spot exchange rate), interest rates, and the income accruing on the foreign currency. (The income accruing on a particular currency is, of course, the income that could be earned on an investment in that currency.)

Take, as an example, the Japanese yen measured against the U.S. dollar. Suppose that today you are able to buy 150 yen (¥150) for one dollar. In other words, the spot rate for the purchase of yen is ¥150 = $1. Suppose further that you have $1 to invest for a period of one year. Now you have a choice. You might either invest the $1 dollar directly—say, in a deposit with a U.S. bank—or you might (assuming no regulatory impediments) convert the dollar into yen and deposit the yen for one year. At the same time as you deposit the yen, you would utilize the forward foreign exchange market to lock-in a forward yen/dollar exchange rate, at which you would sell your yen principal and interest in return for dollars.

By undertaking these transactions, you will have locked-in the number of dollars to be received at the end of one year. For an investment of $1 you will, after one year, receive a dollar amount which will not change as a function of the yen/dollar spot rate. You will, in other words, have locked-in a dollar rate of return and, though your deposit was actually made in yen, you will not suffer if the yen depreciates against the dollar. In the jargon of finance, you have *hedged* your yen investment back into dollars.

As a money manager, you are faced daily with problems similar to the following: suppose the one-year forward rate for selling yen in exchange for dollars is ¥140 = $1. In other words, you can contract today to sell ¥140 for $1, for payment and delivery one year hence. Suppose also that the one-year dollar interest rate is 8% p.a. and the one-year yen interest rate is 5% p.a. What strategy would you be best advised to follow in order to maximize the dollar yield of a one-year investment? Should you invest the dollar directly, or should you instead buy yen spot, deposit the yen at 5% p.a., and utilize the forward foreign exchange market to sell the maturing yen principal and interest in order to lock-in a dollar yield? The alternative cash flows are set out in Figure 5–1.

Figure 5–1

	Alternative 1	Alternative 2
Year	**Invest Dollars**	**Invest Yen**
0 (Spot)	Invest $1 at 8% p.a.	Buy $1 worth of yen at spot rate of ¥150 = $1 and invest the ¥150 at 5% p.a.
1	Receive repayment of principal and interest aggregating $1.08	(i) Receive repayment of yen principal and interest aggregating ¥157.50 and (ii) sell for dollars at the forward rate of ¥140 = $1. Dollars received thus = $1.125
Total dollar interest received	$0.08	$0.125

From Figure 5–1, it emerges that, despite the fact that yen interest rates are only 5% p.a. compared with 8% p.a. in dollars, it makes the most sense for the investor to exchange dollars for yen, invest the yen, and lock-in a dollar repayment amount using the forward foreign exchange market. Since the two alternatives are not economically identical—that is, since they entail differing rewards despite identical risk—there is an arbitrage opportunity.

We can use the arbitrage pricing method to find the unique forward foreign exchange rate which will eliminate the arbitrage opportunity. Like all no-arbitrage forward exchange rates, this 'correct' rate will be a function of the spot exchange rate and interest rates prevailing in each of the two currencies. The no-arbitrage forward rate will be that at which an investor will finish with the same number of dollars, whether he invests $1 directly or through yen. In the above example, this unique forward rate will be ¥157.50 = $1.08, or ¥145.83 = $1.

If yen deposits only earn 5% p.a., compared with 8% p.a. in dollars, the interest rate deficit entailed by investing in yen must be compensated by appreciation in the yen relative to the dollar, as reflected in the forward foreign exchange rate. The yen, that will roll-off from the yen deposit in the form of principal and interest one year hence, will need to be more valuable, in dollar terms, than the yen that are placed on deposit today.

Such appreciation, of course, is not to be expected only of the Japanese yen. The general rule illustrated by the yen example is that all low interest rate currencies will trade at a premium to higher interest rate currencies in the forward foreign exchange market. This rule is of crucial importance to the corporate Treasurer and investment professional and, indeed, applies to forward and futures prices in any commodity. In the case of stocks, for example, the rule is that the break-even forward price of a share of stock will be higher than the spot price of the share if the dividend yield is lower than the prevailing interest rate, and vice versa.

USING THE FORWARD PRICING EQUATION TO DETERMINE FORWARD FOREIGN EXCHANGE RATES

The expanded general forward and futures pricing equation (Equation 4(1)) can be used to compute the 'correct', no-arbitrage forward exchange rate of ¥145.83 = $1 derived in the example cited above. In using the equation, however, we must be careful to work consistently in one currency; bear in mind the methodology by which Equation 4(1) is derived. A dollar deposit of $1 will 'cost' $1. The replicating portfolio consists of a yen deposit, also costing $1, plus a forward foreign exchange contract by which the amount of the maturing yen deposit is sold in exchange for dollars. The yen deposit matures in an amount equal to its principal, plus interest computed at 5% p.a. Hence, in applying Equation 4(1) the variables will be interpreted as follows:

f will be the no-arbitrage forward value, expressed in dollars, of the ¥150 of principal from the maturing yen deposit;

r will be the prevailing dollar interest rate per compounding period, i.e., 8% p.a.;

n will be the number of compounding periods up to the forward date, i.e., one compounding period of one year;

S will be the spot cost of the ¥150 deposit, expressed in dollars, i.e., $1;

CF_j will be the 5% of interest earned on the deposit portion of the replicating portfolio in the *j*th—the one and only—compounding period, i.e., $0.05;

R is the discount rate by which it is appropriate to present value the cash flows associated with the yen deposit. It is, of course, appropriate to present value a yen cash flow using a yen discount rate, hence *R* is 5% p.a.; and

c is the no-arbitrage price of the forward contract, which is zero.

Thus, applying Equation 4(1):

$$f = (1.08)^1 \times \left[1 - \frac{0.05}{(1.05)^1}\right]$$

$$= 1.0286$$

The 'correct' forward rate, then, is ¥150 = $1.0286, or ¥145.83 = $1.

BOND FUTURES: WHAT THE YIELD CURVE SAYS ABOUT FUTURE AND FORWARD INTEREST RATES

The forward and futures pricing equations developed in the foregoing sections can, of course, be applied to the valuation of bond futures as well as to forward positions in BMWs or currencies, or to stock futures. A bond is a piece of paper that entitles the holder to receive cash payments of interest through its life and to repayment of principal at the bond's maturity.

The yield of a bond with a far-off or "long" maturity is normally higher than that of a bond with a shorter maturity. This difference in yield is in part attributable to the increased credit risk entailed by holding a long-term investment, rather than a short-term investment. The *yield curve* is a graph which describes the relationship between bond yields, which are marked on the *y*-axis, and bond maturities, which are marked on the *x*-axis. A "positive" yield curve describes the normal situation in which an increase in maturity is accompanied by an increase in yield. When, for whatever reason, short-term yields are higher than long-term yields, an "inverse" yield curve is said to exist. (See Figure 5–2.)

A great deal has been said over the years about what factors influence the shape of the yield curve. One of these factors, for example, might be investors' beliefs about whether yields will rise or fall in the future. If you are a rational bond investor and believe yields will fall, then you will be inclined to invest in bonds with long maturities, because they enable you to enjoy today's high rate of interest for a long period. Conversely, if you believe rates will rise, then you will be inclined to invest for a short period, in anticipation of early switching into higher yielding investments. This buying pressure at the "short end" will tend to depress yields on short maturity bonds relative to long maturity bonds and thus to steepen the slope of the yield curve.

Whatever an investor may believe about the direction in which interest rates are headed, there is nevertheless a 'correct', no-arbitrage price for a futures position in a specific bond at any point in time. In Chapter 2, we saw that, given its pre-determined repayment schedule and coupon (interest rate), the yield of a bond is a function of its market price. The lower the market price of the bond (that is, the lower the original investment needed to acquire the bond and the cash flows to which it represents title), the higher its yield (i.e, the higher the return on that original investment). Knowing the

Figure 5–2 U.S. Government Bond Yield Curve as of Mid-Afternoon on November 28, 1990

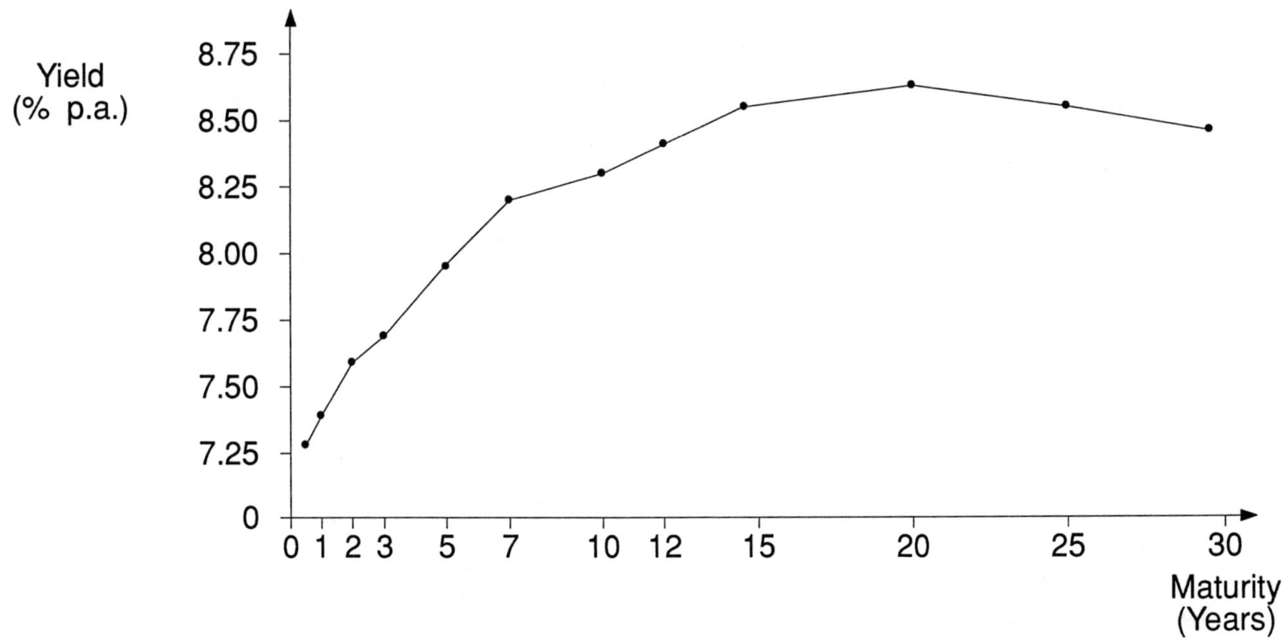

appropriate yield of a specific bond, we can also derive the bond's appropriate market price. Yield is a crucial concept, not only to investors (to whom it is an alternate measure of the price of the bonds they own), but also to financial managers, to whom it represents a measure of the cost of raising money through the sale of a bond issue.

As we saw in Chapter 2, the price of a bond is the aggregate of the present values of each of the cash flows associated with that bond, each discounted at the bond's yield. Suppose the market yield for top quality twenty-year bonds in the cash market (i.e., for spot payment and delivery) is 8% p.a. If the coupon attaching to a top quality twenty-year bond is 8% p.a. and the bond has a $100 principal value, then using Equation 2(2), we can show that the price of the bond is—not surprisingly—$100. Now, suppose that we have a positive yield curve in which the yield on top quality one-year bonds in the cash market is 7% p.a., i.e., 1% p.a. below the twenty-year yield. Equipped with this information, we can find the 'correct' one-year forward price for a top quality twenty-year bond (or a 19-year bond, as it will be by the time it is delivered under the forward contract).

Following our practice in earlier arbitrage pricing exercises, the first step is to think about how the cash purchase of a twenty-year bond might be replicated using such a one-year forward contract, a 'rental' arrangement, plus some sort of a borrowing or lending strategy. The forward contract will confer all the cash flows associated with an 8% p.a. twenty-year bond purchased in the cash market, except for the first year's coupon payment of $8. This first year's coupon is what an investor will forego by buying the forward contract (and simultaneously investing the PV of the forward price so that he is ready to pay the forward price when the time comes), rather than the cash twenty-year bond. The investor will thus have to invest the PV of this $8 at today's one-year interest rate of 7% p.a. in order to replicate the missing coupon. So, the replicating portfolio comprises (i) the forward contract, (ii) a one-year investment which matures in an amount equal to the forward price, and (iii) a one-year investment which matures in an amount of \$8. In order that there should be no arbitrage opportunity the aggregate cost of these three components of the replicating portfolio must equal the cash price of the twenty-year bond:

$$c + \frac{f}{(1.07)^1} + \frac{\$8}{(1.07)^1} = \$100$$

If $c = \$0$ then $f = \$99$.

The equivalence of the two positions—that is, of the cash bond on the one hand and the replicating portfolio on the other—can be shown by simply tabulating the cash flows associated with each (see Figure 5–3).

Again, we can arrive at the same result using the expanded general forward and futures pricing equation (Equation 4(1)). In this application, S is the cash price of the twenty-year bond (i.e., \$100); CF_j is the income earned on the underlying commodity the twenty-year bond—up to the delivery date (i.e., \$8); r and R are the one-year discount rates used to determine the PV of f and CF_j, respectively (which, since we are dealing with an instrument of the highest quality, are each 7% p.a.); and n is the one year up to the futures date. Thus:

$$f = (1.07)^1 \times \left[\$100 - \frac{\$8}{(1.07)^1} \right]$$

$$= \$99$$

At this price, what will be the yield of a bond with nineteen years of remaining life on the delivery date? This question can

Figure 5–3

	Cash Flows				
Year	Buy Cash Bond	=	Pay Futures Price, Hold Bond	+	Make Deposit of $100
Today	<$100>				<$100>
1	$8		<$99>		$107
2–19	$8		$8		
20	$108		$108		

be answered by applying Equation 2(2) and solving for r. In this case, $r = 8.10\%$ p.a.

Like forward foreign exchange rates, we can readily explain why the forward bond should have a yield of 0.10% p.a. in excess of the cash twenty-year bond yield. If we are to replicate a twenty-year bond yielding 8% p.a. using a forward contract plus a deposit which yields just 7%, the forward position must yield more than 8% p.a. to bring the overall yield on the replicating portfolio up to the 8% p.a. of the cash bond. When the interest or discount rate for the period up to a delivery date is lower than the yield on a commodity, then a forward or futures position in that commodity must be priced at a discount to the commodity's cash or spot price, and vice versa. In the case of bonds, this means that so long as we have a positive yield curve, a bond forward or futures contract—

one providing for forward payment and delivery—will be priced at a discount to (i.e., will have a higher yield than) the cash bond.

A NOTE ON CASH-FORWARD AND CASH-FUTURES ARBITRAGE

Whenever an arbitrage opportunity exists as a result of a misalignment between cash and forward prices, or between a cash price and the price of a particular forward or futures contract, then that arbitrage opportunity is referred to as a *cash-forward* or *cash-futures* arbitrage opportunity. Today a huge volume of activity on major futures and stock exchanges in accounted for by cash-futures arbitrage trading, including program trading. 'Program trading' normally denotes cash-futures arbitrages in stock index futures contracts. Brokerage houses will automatically monitor for cash-futures misalignments and, where misalignments arise, will automatically generate the appropriate buy and sell transactions to exploit the opportunity.

While this sort of program trading came under fire for its possible aggravating effect on the October 1987 stock market crash, it clearly enhances efficiency by improving the harmony between markets. This book is not, however, the forum in which to undertake a review of the morality of this sort of trading in light of its implications for, for example, the small investor.

Chapter 6

6

Discounting and Arbitrage Pricing at Work

THE FREQUENT FLYER PROGRAM

You are treasurer of a corporation employing 250 sales and customer relations staff. These staff travel regularly and, because of the distribution of their calls, all invariably use the same airline. Under the circumstances, you believe that enrolling the sales and customer service staff in the airline's frequent flyer program may prove a useful perk. The three-year group enrollment cost for your staff would be $5,000.

On the basis of the coming years' travel schedules, however, you believe that none of the staff will qualify for a mileage award within one year and that after one year, only 150 of the staff will qualify for the lowest award—a cut-price ticket award, worth about $25. During the third year, after which membership of the program lapses, 210 of the staff will qualify for the lowest award. The question is whether the enrollment in the frequent flyer program is worth the $5,000 fee involved, or whether there is a better way to spend $5,000 on your staff.

The first step is to tabulate cash flows. Enrolling the staff in the frequent flyer program would produce costs and awards as set out in Figure 6–1.

The mileage awards can only be redeemed on the airline sponsoring the frequent flyer program. The risk of the airline going out of business before expiration of your staff's membership, you believe, is about the same as the risk of the First Bank of Thirdton going out of business within two years. First Bank is paying a maximum of 9% p.a. on one- and two-year uninsured deposits. A question, therefore, is whether the cash flows associated with the frequent flyer program have a yield exceeding 9% p.a—in which case the mileage program would

Figure 6–1

Year	Costs and Benefits—$ Value	
0—today	($5,000)	[Enrollment cost]
1	$3,750	[150 awards at $25 each]
2	$5,250	[210 awards at $25 each]

be a reasonable investment relative to a deposit with First Bank—or lower than 9% p.a.—in which case a $5,000 deposit with First Bank for the benefit of your employees would make more economic sense.

The best way to tackle this question may not be actually to find the internal rate of return, or yield, of the frequent flyer cash flows. This is an iterative process and may only make sense if you have a calculator capable of performing yield computations. The optimal way of approaching the question may simply be to discount the value of the anticipated mileage awards at the First Bank deposit rate of 9% p.a., using Equation 2(1). If they have an aggregate present value which exceeds $5,000, then the mileage program will be a better investment than the First Bank deposit:

PV of $3,750, discounted over 1 year at 9% p.a = $\$3{,}750/(1.09)^1 = \$3{,}440.37$

PV of $5,250, discounted over 2 years at 9% p.a. = $\$5{,}250/(1.09)^2 = \$4{,}418.82$

Thus, the aggregate PV of the anticipated mileage awards is $7,859.19, which is a full $2,859.19 more than the alternative $5,000 deposit with First Bank. The mileage program, therefore, is an attractive investment, relative to the deposit.

THE CASE OF THE BULL AND BEAR BOND ISSUES

The 1980s were a notable decade so far as financial markets were concerned. The great bull market of the mid-80s gave rise to a taste for new and exotic financial instruments. Among the innovations, 1986 saw the development of a market for what were picturesquely labeled "bull and bear," or sometimes (even more picturesquely) "heaven or hell," bonds.

A number of these esoteric bond issues were sold in a number of different forms. The feature common to all, however, was that as the bonds matured they were to be repaid in an amount which depended on the then prevailing price of a particular commodity, to which the repayment amount was tied or *indexed*. It is illuminating to analyze a hypothetical example of such a bond issue to find out what was going on.

Suppose First Taxpayers' Bank issues a total of $200 face amount of "bull and bear" bonds, all maturing in 3 years. The issue of bonds is divided into two parts—a "bull" part and a "bear" part—each part having a face amount of $100. Both parts of the bond issue are sold at their original face amount, raising $200 for First Taxpayers'.

The "bull" part (or *tranche*) of the bond issue pays interest at 3% p.a. and is repaid in an amount that is tied to the price of one-fifth of an ounce of gold. The indexation is such that if the price of gold at the time of repayment is higher than a certain threshold amount, then the repayment will be higher than the bonds' original face amount, and vice versa. The threshold gold price is $600 per ounce, reflected in the formula for determining the bull bonds' repayment amount:

> Repayment per $100 original face amount = $100 + $(1/5) \times (G - \$600)$, subject to a maximum repayment of $200 and a minimum repayment of $0.

In this formula, *G* is the prevailing spot price of one ounce of gold on the bonds' maturity date. Thus, if the gold price were to rise to $750 per ounce on the maturity date, then the repayment per $100 of original face amount of bull bonds would be $130. Conversely, if the spot price were to fall to $400 per ounce, then the repayment would fall to just $60 per $100 original face amount.

It is not difficult to see why this tranche of the bond issue should be termed the "bull" tranche. The natural buyers of the bull bonds—other than arbitrageurs who perceived riskless arbitrage opportunities—would be those who held bullish expectations for the gold price. Those, in other words, who were anticipating a rise in the price of gold and thus repayment of the bonds at a premium to their original face amount.

The second, "bear" tranche of the bond issue pays a coupon of 10% p.a. and is to be repaid in an amount which is inversely correlated to the price of one-fifth of an ounce of gold. In this case, however, the threshold gold price is $500 per ounce—so to the extent the gold price falls below $500 per ounce the bear bonds repay more than their original face amount, and vice versa. The repayment formula is:

> Repayment per $100 original face amount = $100 - (1/5) × (*G* - $500), subject to a maximum repayment of $200 and a minimum repayment of $0.

Again, *G* is the spot price of one ounce of gold prevailing on the bonds' maturity date.

The first thing that should be emphasized is that, having issued the bull and bear bonds together, First Taxpayers' Bank is not exposed to the gold price. Whatever the price of gold may be in three years time (that is, whatever *G* may turn out to be), the issuer's total repayment obligation remains the same. This can be demonstrated simply by adding the two repayment formulae:

> Total repayment = bull bond repayment + bear bond repayment

$$= [\$100 + (1/5) \times (G\text{-}\$600)] + [\$100 - (1/5) \times (G - \$500)]$$

$$= \$180$$

For the $100 original face amount of bull plus the $100 original face amount of bear bonds, therefore, the issuer's cash flows are as set out in Figure 6–2.

The internal rate of return of the issuer's total cash flow is 3.27% p.a. This is the effective cost of the money raised by Third Taxpayers' through the issue of the bull and bear bonds. Now 3.27% p.a. is, in the context of the interest rate environment that has prevailed in recent years, an attractive financing cost. Suppose, for example, that First Taxpayers' would have to pay interest at about 8% p.a. if it were to undertake an issue of conventional three-year bonds. The question then arises, who is subsidizing First Taxpayers' to the tune of 4.73% p.a. in connection with the bull and bear bonds? Are the buyers of the bull bonds getting a raw deal, or is it the buyers of the bear bonds who are bearing the brunt of the issuer's saving, or is it both? To value the bull and bear bonds, we need to take them apart and look at their composition.

Valuing the Bull Bonds

How might the cash flows associated with the bull bonds be replicated using easy-to-value components? The bull bond pays interest, albeit at the low rate of 3% p.a. It also repays its original face amount plus or minus something, where the "something" depends on the then prevailing gold price. So we can analyze the bull bond as a 3% p.a. conventional bond plus an instrument which entitles the investor to plus or minus "something." The question thus becomes how to replicate and value this instrument?

The "something" is one-fifth of the amount by which the gold price varies from $600 per ounce three years hence. Consider how this resembles the profit or loss from an unhedged three-year forward position in one-fifth of an ounce of gold, where the forward price is $600 per ounce. If an

Figure 6–2

Year	Cash Flows Bull Bond	+	Bear Bond	=	Total
0	$100		$100		$200
1	<$3>		<$10>		<$13>
2	<$3>		<$10>		<$13>
3	<$100 – (1/5) × (*G* – $600)> +<$3>		<$100 – (1/5) × (*G* – $500)> +<$10>		<$193>

investor contracts to buy one-fifth of an ounce of gold three years hence at a forward price of \$600 per ounce, he will profit if the then-prevailing gold price—*G*—exceeds \$600 per ounce at the delivery date. If the then-prevailing price is, say, \$800 he will find himself, pursuant to the forward contract, paying \$120 for one-fifth of an ounce which has a then current spot market value of \$160—a clear \$40 profit. Conversely, if the then prevailing gold price is just \$400 per ounce, the forward buyer will be paying \$120 for a commodity with a then current spot market value of just \$80—a \$40 loss. With respect to this hypothetical forward position, we can express the forward buyer's profit as a function of the prevailing spot price of gold at the three-year delivery date, *G*:

$$\text{forward profit} = (1/5) \times (G - \$600)$$

Now, if we add this hypothetical forward position profit (which will be negative—a loss—if $G < \$600$) to the repayment of a conventional 3% p.a. three-year bond with an original face value of \$100, we have a total repayment of:

$$\$100 + (1/5) \times (G - \$600)$$

This amount, you will notice, is identical to the repayment associated with \$100 original face amount of bull bonds. The bull bonds' replicating portfolio, therefore, comprises (i) a conventional 3% p.a. three-year bond, and (ii) a three-year forward position in one-fifth of an ounce of gold with forward price of \$600 per ounce. We can now value these elements:

(i) The bond component has a value which is the aggregate of the PVs of each of the bond's cash flows, discounted at the appropriate rate. This appropriate rate will reflect the risk associated with First Taxpayers' and will be approximately equal to First Taxpayers' three-year bond rate of 8% p.a.[1]

The value of the bond component can be calculated using Equation 2(2):

$$\textit{bond value} = \frac{\$3}{(1+0.08)^1} + \frac{\$3}{(1+0.08)^2} + \frac{\$103}{(1+0.08)^3}$$

$$= \$87.11$$

(ii) The forward gold component of the replicating portfolio can be valued by reference to the expanded general forward and futures pricing equation, Equation 4(1), and solving for c. Note, that in Equation 4(1), CF_j represents the cash flow associated with the underlying commodity—in this case gold—in compounding period j. Since gold is a non-income bearing commodity, CF_j in this case is equal to 0. Hence:

$$f = (1+r)^3 \times (S - c)$$

In buying the bull bonds, an investor's receipt of the "something" which is replicated by the forward contract, has First Taxpayers' risk attaching to it. Hence, for the purpose of

---

[1] I say "approximately equal to" because, strictly speaking, the appropriate discount rate to use here may be other than 8% p.a. The reason is that, as we have discussed, bond yields and discount rates tend to differ, depending on the maturity of the bond. Typically an investment that is at risk longer will earn a higher yield. First Taxpayers' 8% p.a. bond rate no doubt reflects the risk associated with a "current coupon" bond which pays interest at the full market level of 8% p.a. Such a bond will have a shorter *duration* than a bond which pays interest at just 3 % p.a. and which is priced at a discount to reflect this low interest rate. Why? Because after two years the current coupon bond has already paid back, by way of coupon payments, $16 of the invertor's original outlay. The "deep discount" bond, meanwhile, will have paid back a proportionally smaller amount of its purchase price after two years. Most of a discount bond's return comes only at its maturity, rolled-up in its repayment, which is high relative to its original purchase price.

this equation, the discount rate, r, should also reflect First Taxpayers' risk and will thus be 8% p.a. Thus:

$$c = S - \frac{f}{(1.08)^3}$$

Suppose that the spot price of gold is $520 per ounce. S—the spot price of the underlying commodity (one-fifth of an ounce of gold)—will thus be $104. Hence:

$$c = \$104 - \frac{\$120}{(1.08)^3} = \$8.74$$

Adding the values of the two component elements comprising the bull bonds' replicating portfolio, we arrive at a value for the bull bonds themselves (since the value of a replicating portfolio equals the value of that which it replicates) of $87.11 + $8.74, or $95.85. Investors, who are being offered the bonds at their original face value of $100 are, therefore, being overcharged by approximately $4.15.

Valuing the Bear Bonds

Like the bull bonds, the first component of the bear bonds is a conventional three-year bond, this time paying a coupon of 10% p.a. Its face value, calculated using Equation 2(2), is $105.15. The gold indexation of the bear bonds, however, reflects an inverse correlation between the gold price and an the repayment amount; the investor loses if the gold price rises (this time, above $500 per ounce) and profits if the gold price falls. While, for the investor, the bull bonds represented in part a purchase of a forward position in gold—that is, a *long* forward position—the bear bonds represent the sale of a forward position in gold—that is, a *short* forward position.

Consider the effect of contracting to sell one fifth of an ounce of gold three years hence at a forward price of $100 per ounce. If the gold price three years hence—*G*—has risen to $800 it will cost you $160 to buy one-fifth of an ounce of gold in the spot market. When you deliver this pursuant to the forward contract, however, all you receive in return is the $100 forward price, leaving you with a $60 loss. Conversely, if the gold price has fallen to $400 you will deliver, in return for the $100 forward price, one-fifth of an ounce which will have a spot market value of $80. This leaves you in the happy position of having realized a $20 profit. We can express the profit of this short forward position as a function of *G*:

$$\text{short forward profit} = (1/5) \times (\$500 - G)$$

or, alternatively,

$$\text{short forward profit} = -\,(1/5) \times (G - \$500)$$

This, of course, is part of the repayment formula associated with the bear bonds.

Just as with the bull bonds, we can use Equation 4(1) to value the three-year short forward position in one-fifth of an ounce of gold:

$$-\,c \text{ [where the minus sign signifies the short]}$$

$$= \$104 - \frac{\$100}{(1.08)^3} = \$24.62$$

Hence

$$c = -\,\$24.62$$

Taking the value of the bond component and adding the negative value associated with the short forward component of the bear bonds, therefore, we arrive at a value for the bear bonds of just $80.53. Investors in the bear bonds, despite the bear bonds' superior interest rate of 10% p.a., are being grossly overcharged.

We have valued the bull bonds and the bear bonds and determined that the former are slightly overpriced, while the latter are grossly overpriced. We can now perform a quick cross-check on our valuation, for if the bonds were marketed at their fair values, no investor would be subsidizing First Taxpayers' and, similarly, First Taxpayers' would be subsidizing no investor. In other words, First Taxpayers' aggregate cash flows associated with the two tranches of bonds would have an internal rate of return equal to First Taxpayers' conventional bond rate of 8% p.a., as indeed they do (see Figure 6–3).

There is just one thing that remains to be said concerning our analysis: note that it omits any consideration of the limits—the cap of $200 and the floor of zero—placed upon the repayment amounts associated with each tranche of bonds. If we wished to complete the analysis we would have to account for these limits by throwing options into the basket of replicating instruments. However, since options are the subject of coming chapters, and since this would unduly complicate our present analysis, such a refinement is as well omitted here.

Figure 6–3

	Cash Flows				
Year	**Bull Bond**	+	**Bear Bond**	=	**Total**
0	$95.85		$80.53		$176.38
1	<$3>		<$10>		<$13>
2	<$3>		<$10>		<$13>
3	<$100 – (1/5) × (*G* – $600)> +<$3>		<$100 – (1/5) × (*G* – $500)> +<$10>		<$193>
			IRR:		8% p.a.

Chapter 7

7

Risk and Reward: the Fundamental Relationship

RISK

Risk is a function of probabilities. It is also a function of possible loss. Someone who advises you, "don't walk alone through that part of town late at night, it's risky," is telling you that there is an appreciable (to him, an unacceptably high) probability that something unpleasant will happen to you if you do. He might try to put a number on the risk. For example, ask him what he means when he says it's risky to walk alone, and he might reply: "Well, there's a one-in-five chance [i.e., a 20% probability] you'll be mugged if you do." To talk of the risk associated with some plan or investment is to talk in part about the degree of confidence you have that things will turn out as you anticipate and in part about what you stand to lose if they don't. The more confidence you have or the less you stand to lose the lower the risk you ascribe and vice versa.

THE DIE GAME: AN EXERCISE IN ARBITRAGE PRICING

After dinner with several friends, one of the guests turns to you holding a die. This guest offers $300 to anyone who correctly guesses what face will turn up on the next throw. How much of a stake—that is, what kind of an investment—should you be willing to put up to participate in the game? Put another way, what is the fair value of the *contingent* entitlement to receive $300? The entitlement to the $300 is, of course, contingent in the sense that even if you put up the requisite stake you will only receive the prize if you guess correctly which face will be thrown.

You want to be in the die game and you want to back the number three. Knowing your friend to be honest, you have full confidence the die is unbiased—that is, you do not believe your friend to have any reason to believe any particular face is more likely to be thrown than any other. You thus infer that there is a one in six (or 16⅔%) probability that a 3 will be thrown. It is likely that almost intuitively it will seem to you that the fair stake to back your chosen number 3 should be $50, for the fair stake is the potential payoff, or prize, multiplied by the probability that it will be received. This is the relationship, after all, embodied in the concept of 'odds'. If five horses are running in the three o'clock race at Belmont and they are perfectly matched, then each (in a perfect world in which bookmakers' profits are eliminated) will carry odds of five to one. This means that for a one-dollar stake your payoff will be five times one dollar in the event your horse wins.

We will call this relationship between a stake, the associated probability of a win, and the payoff in the event of a win, the *basic price-payoff relationship*. It is the key to the determination of the 'fair' price to put at risk in anticipation of a payoff which is in any way contingent upon what happens in the future. But how is the basic price-payoff relationship derived? Is it simply axiomatic, or is there some other reason why, in the die game, \$50 (i.e., 16⅔% of \$300) is the fair stake for a bet on the number three? After all, if you lose in the game—and you are five times more likely to lose than to win—you will have lost \$50, and who can say, "well, it was worth it"?

The basic price-payoff relationship can, in fact, be derived using, among other things, an arbitrage pricing methodology. The reason that \$50 is the fair stake for your bet on the number three is that, under certain circumstances, any stake lower than \$50 would enable you to make a guaranteed profit, while any stake higher than \$50 would guarantee you a loss. To illustrate this, suppose your friend offered to take your bet on the number three for \$40. To exploit this apparent mispricing, you and five others around the dinner table could form a syndicate. Each member of the syndicate would join the die game and would bet on a different face so that the syndicate had all six die faces covered. The syndicate, as a group, is bound to win the \$300 prize money since, neglecting the (remote) possibility of the die landing and balancing on an edge, one of the six faces is bound to be thrown. If the aggregate of the stakes put up is less than \$300, then the syndicate is guaranteed a profit. To use the conventional terminology introduced earlier in the book, we can say that an *arbitrage opportunity* exists. If each face were covered for a $40 stake—meaning the syndicate had laid out $240 in all—the arbitrage profit would be $60.

In a rational market no vendor, whether of bets or anything else, will price his commodities so that his customers are guaranteed to come out ahead at his (the vendor's) expense. In Chapter 3—as throughout this book—'correct', or 'fair', prices for commodities are derived using the arbitrage pricing method, by which we try to identify how arbitrage strategies may be structured and price our commodity so as to eliminate the profit potential. The arbitrage pricing method entails finding, in other words, the price at which the purchase of a commodity and the sale of a replicating portfolio becomes a zero-sum game.

ONE OMISSION AND ONE CAVEAT

Omission: the Concept of 'Fairness'

The observant reader of the die game scenario will have detected a hidden assumption at work in deriving the fair stake using the arbitrage pricing method. For what does the arbitrage pricing method really tell us about the fair pricing of bets in the game? It tells us that only if all faces of the die were covered for an aggregate stake of $300—the amount of the prize on offer—would the whole exercise be bound to be a zero-sum game. This is all that arbitrage pricing *can* tell us. It can tell us nothing about the value of a bet on any one face of the die. So what makes a bet on the number three worth $50? If, for example, a bet on the number three were on offer for $10, still no *riskless* arbitrage opportunity would exist so long as the bets on all the other five faces were on offer for an aggregate of $290. If bets on each of the other five faces were on offer for $58 each, for example, no syndicate could be formed that would be guaranteed a profit.

So, why is the fair price of a bet on the number 3 not $10 or indeed anything else? The answer to the question has to do with the concept of 'fairness'.

The assertion that "the 'fair' (no-arbitrage) aggregate of stakes in the die game is $300" entails the assertion that "the 'fair' stake for a bet on any individual face is $50" only if we hold that a bet on any one face should be priced the same as a bet on any other face. The only basis for this suggestion can be that a bet on any one face is, in a sense, identical to a bet on any other face. If you were allowed to back the number three for a $10 stake, another dinner guest might argue that he should be allowed to back the number five for a $10 stake. He would claim this right because the number three and the number five are equally likely to be thrown. Since the bets are in this sense identical, then the cost of those bets—the stakes—should also be identical. We will call this line of reasoning the *fairness argument*. The user of the argument will hold that the guest offering the $300 prize is, in effect, selling contingent entitlements to the prize and that those contingent entitlements are identical commodities which, because they are identical, should be sold at identical prices.

Caveat: the Concept of 'Prudence'

Imagine you are the general manager of a computer retailing company. One of your marketing people is arguing that his budget should be increased to allow solicitation of a potential new customer with a $2 million new equipment requirement. The gross profit from such a sale would be $120,000. Your man tells you that he is, "absolutely certain to close this deal," provided that he is given the substantial amounts of cash and other resources the marketing exercise would entail. This somewhat exaggerated statement (exaggerated because there is no such thing as absolute certainty where marketing is concerned) is reflective of a high degree of confidence, which you share, that the deal would, given the marketing investment, be closed. Suppose that you ascribe an 80% probability to the closing. In the 20% chance that the sale fails to close, of course, the substantial marketing investment will need to be written-off. What is the maximum amount that you should be willing to commit in pursuit of this business?

The similarity between this question and "What is the fair stake to be put up in the die game?" should be readily apparent. In both the die game and the computer retailing game, the question arises whether an investment of such-and-such is justified in light of the assessed probability of winning, on the one hand, and the prize on offer, on the other. But a crude application of the basic price-payoff relationship to the computer marketing problem would suggest that a marketing budget of up to $96,000—the 80% assessed probability of winning the business multiplied by the $120,000 gross profit to be had if the business is won—should be reasonable or fair. This result may well prove counter-intuitive to a prudent and conservative businessman. It has this appearance because proper business decision-making is not quite so straightforward as applying the simple mathematical model we currently have at our disposal.

For one thing, we have ignored the time value of money. While the marketing expense is incurred up-front, the payoff would come only on signing of the purchase and sale contract—say, three months down the road. A present value adjustment should thus be made to take timing differences into account. Much more important, however, is that sensible decision-making must involve a proper regard for the demands of *prudence*. The basic price-payoff relationship is not all there is to the decision whether this or that potential outcome should be backed. There is always a limit to what it may be prudent to put at risk, no matter how attractive the odds on offer.

The fact that the basic price-payoff relationship can be used to derive 'fair' prices, but not necessarily those prices that we *should* pay (which will be a function also of 'prudence'), reflects the two-stage nature of buying and other investment decisions. First, the fair value of a thing is derived; this is the maximum price that anyone should reasonably be prepared to pay for the thing. Second, whether to pay up to that fair value for the thing will depend upon certain of the potential buyer's individual circumstances.[1]

It should be noted that the concept of prudence does not serve to undermine the analogy between business decisions and gambling decisions. A gambler would be imprudent and ill-advised to stake all on a long-shot, whether or not he liked the odds; in just the same way, a business would be ill-advised to take such a cavalier approach with its shareholders' equity. The distaste many businessmen appear to feel for the notion that what they do is closely related to what gamblers do probably springs from a neglect of this fact. It is, indeed, a fact which is easy to miss, because the word "gambling" has come not only to denote a class of activities which involve putting something at risk in anticipation of a future payoff, but also to carry overtones of recklessness and imprudence.

Most businesses rightly and prudently shy away from risks which exceed a certain level. The ceiling level of acceptable risk will tend to be lower for a bank, for example, than it will be for a high-growth electronics company, whose stockholders expect it to take substantial risks in furtherance of its growth. Ceiling risk cannot be computed. It is a matter for managers and shareholders, or gamblers and their families and bankers, to work out between themselves.

There are further caveats to be introduced when considering the viability and applicability of the models—including

[1] More of this under "Marginal Utility" in Chapter 16.

option pricing models—which embody the basic price-payoff relationship. The subjectivity of probability ascriptions and the concept of marginal utility are discussed in Chapter 16. It should be noted that these caveats are of more than purely philosophical interest, because in financial markets huge sums are customarily invested on the basis of deviations between the actual price of a particular commodity and its 'fair' price, as determined using these models. It is only with the pricing models derived from the basic price-payoff relationship in one hand and an appreciation of the logical status of the results of their application in the other that you will be fully equipped to determine the optimal path at any decision crossroads.

THE SCOPE OF CONTINGENT CONTRACT PRICING

It has already been described how bets are contingent in the sense that, having paid some stake up-front, still the realization of a payoff remains contingent upon future occurrences, such as the number three being thrown in the die game, or your horse winning in the big race. Of all financial securities, options are the most clearly contingent in nature. An option entitles the holder to buy or sell a particular commodity at a pre-determined price. The profit that an option-holder will receive from the exercise of this right will depend upon the price of the underlying commodity at such future point in time as he decides or is able to exercise the option. For example, if an option confers the right to buy a share of stock at a price of $100 and the market price of the share when the investor comes to exercise this right is $110, then the investor's effective profit is $10, less the purchase price of the option. He is buying for $100 something which he can immediately turn around and sell in the open market for $110. But if the market price of the share turns out to be just $90, then the investor will be out of pocket the option's purchase price. He will simply throw the option away unexercised, for it would obviously be irrational of him to choose to buy for $100 by way of the option what he could buy in the open market for just $90. By its terms, then, the profit received from an option is wholly contingent upon what happens to the price of the underlying commodity. It is far from a contractually specified number of dollars and cents.

Bonds, on the other hand (or at least, most of them), do specify the number of dollars and cents the bondholder is entitled to receive from his investment. Nevertheless, an issuer of bonds might default on his obligation to make principal and interest payments. A low credit rating means that the probability of such a default has been assessed as being appreciable. Hence, even in the case of bonds, the actual amounts to be received from a particular investment are less than 100% certain.

While options—like bets—evidence what we have described as contingent entitlements, bonds can be said to evidence contractual entitlements which are contingently realized. Pragmatic investors are interested in entitlements only to the extent they affect their confidence in being paid. Realizations, not entitlements, are what really count. Any instrument about which there is any doubt as to what will be paid is generally referred to as a "contingent contract." Just as with bets, the value of options, bonds, and all other contingent contracts is a function of the probability of future events occurring—of the price of the underlying stock rising, or the issuing company remaining solvent. Just as with bets, the function embodies the basic price-payoff relationship.

Chapter 8

8

The Do-It-Yourself Option Pricing Model: a Marriage of Finance and Gaming Theory

VALUING AN OPTION AS A PORTFOLIO OF BETS

With a brief analysis of risk and reward behind us and a more rigorous 'academic' analysis of option pricing lying ahead, let's take a moment to devise a very simple, yet perfectly serviceable call option pricing model: the Do-It-Yourself option pricing model. While not the last word in mathematical sophistication, the methodology of this chapter highlights the most important and fundamental relationships between the variables of which the 'fair' option price is a function.

Deriving the Do-It-Yourself option pricing model entails conceiving of any option as a portfolio of bets. The price of a call option on a stock, for example, is to be considered analogous to the stake put up by a gambler. If the stock goes up in price, the call option holder wins. His prize, or payoff,[1] is the then current value of the stock (S) which the option holder receives upon exercise of the option, less the exercise price (E) he has to pay. Formulaically:

$$payoff = S - E$$

As noted in the foregoing chapter, in a game of chance we can derive a fair stake to back a potential outcome. By the basic price-payoff relationship, this fair stake is the product of the prize to be had and the probability of winning. The basic price-payoff relationship lies at the heart of the Do-It-Yourself option pricing model.

Suppose we have a call option which confers the right to buy one share of International Widget stock. The exercise price is equal to the current International Widget share price, which is $100. We can value the call option in five easy steps:

STEP 1: *Make an assessment of probable future prices*

Make your best guess at what the International Widget stock price may be at the time the option lapses (that is, at its *expiration*). You do not have to guess what the exact price *will* be—just assess the probabilities that attach to this potential price and to that potential price. For example, if an Interna-

---

[1] Basic terms—"call," "payoff," and so on—are more fully explained in the following chapter.

tional Widget share is $100 today and has consistently increased in price at 5% p.a., you may believe its single most probable price one year hence is $105. There is a very small probability it will be $80 and a similarly small probability that it will be $130. There is a minor, but appreciable, probability it will be either $90 or $115, and so on. For, say, a one-year option, you might guess at potential future prices as set out in Figure 8–1.

Note that the longer the time to expiration and the more the stock has a tendency to jump around in price (the more *volatile* it is), the more difficult it is to make your guesses. The longer the expiration or greater the volatility, in other words, the more reason you have to ascribe a wide range of potential prices to the International Widget shares one year hence.

STEP 2: *Calculate the payoff for each potential future price*

Figure 8–1

Potential Price, One Year Hence	Probability
Less than $90	5%
$90 – $100	20%
$100 – $110	50%
$110 – $120	20%
over $120	5%

Calculate what the option-holder would receive upon exercise of the option (i.e., calculate the option's payoff) under each of the potential future price scenarios. For simplicity, take the middle-point of each possible price range to compute the payoffs (see Figure 8–2).

STEP 3: *Apply the basic price-payoff relationship*

Owning the International Widget call option is just like owning a bet on each potential future price of the company's shares—one bet on an $85 price, one on a $95 price, one on a $105 price, and so on. If the price turns out to be, say, $115, the holder of the option wins the bet on the $115 price and loses all the other bets. (This is exactly analogous to backing all horses to win in a single race.)

Now the fair stake (C_j) for each of these 'component bets' can be calculated using the basic price-payoff relationship:

Figure 8–2

Future Price	Payoff (i.e., $S - E$)
Less than $90 (say, $85)	$0
$95	$0
$105	$5
$115	$15
Over $120 (say, $130)	$30

C_1 ($85 bet) = Payoff × Probability = $0 × 5% = $0
C_2 ($95 bet) = Payoff × Probability = $0 × 20% = $0
C_3($105 bet) = Payoff × Probability = $5 × 50% = $2.50
C_4($115 bet) = Payoff × Probability = $15 × 20% = $3
C_5($130 bet) = Payoff × Probability = $30 × 5% = $1.50

STEP 4: *Sum the 'fair stakes' for the 'component bets'*

Aggregate fair stake = $0 + $0 + $2.50 + $3 + $1.50 = $7

STEP 5: *Present value the aggregate fair stake*

If you buy the call option you lose access to the purchase price over the period between the option's purchase and its expiration, when you receive the payoff. The aggregate fair stake computed in Step 4 is what you should be willing to pay for an option which gives you an immediate payoff, with no negative time value or opportunity cost. Its present value (discounted at the riskless interest rate) is the value of the option today. Suppose one-year riskless rates are 8% p.a., then

$$\text{fair call option price} = \text{PV of aggregate fair stake}$$

$$= \frac{\$7}{(1.08)^1}$$

$$= \$6.48$$

The five steps described above can be described using a single equation:

$$C = \frac{1}{(1+r)^n} \sum_{j=1}^{N} P_j \times max[(S_j - E), 0]$$

where

C is the fair price of the call option in question;

N is the exhaustive number of possible spot prices of the underlying commodity which might prevail at expiration of the option;

S_j is the jth such possible spot price of the underlying commodity at expiration of the option;

P_j is the probability that the spot price of the underlying commodity prevailing at expiration of the option will be S_j;

E is the exercise price of the call option, and thus $max[(S_j - E), 0]$ (i.e., the higher of $S_j - E$ and 0) is the payoff of the call option in the event of a price outcome of S_j;

r is the annually compounded riskless interest or discounting rate, expressed in % p.a.; and

n is the number of years (i.e., the number of compounding periods) up to the expiration of the option.

Expressed verbally, this equation reads, "the fair value of a call option is equal to the present value of the aggregate of the products of, for each possible payoff of the call, (i) that payoff, and (ii) the probability that it will be obtained."

It should be noted that, for reasons which will emerge in the coming chapter, this equation—this statement of the Do-It-Yourself option pricing model—is valid only in situations where the underlying commodity is non-income bearing.

In order that the rationale underlying the Do-It-Yourself model should be absolutely clear it is as well to work through the five steps in connection with another example. This time suppose we wish to value a one-year call on one International Widget common share, where the exercise price of the call option is $90, compared to the current share price of $100. The volatility of the share price is high and the one-year riskless interest rate is 8% p.a.

STEP 1:

Estimate the probabilities. Note that because the share price volatility is high, there will be a wide range to the prices which may obtain at expiration, as set out in Figure 8–3.

STEPS 2 AND 3:

Compute the payoff and then the fair stake associated with each of the possible future prices (see Figure 8–3).

STEP 4:

Sum the fair stakes:

$$\text{aggregate fair stake} = \$1 + \$4.05 + \$5 + \$4.90 + \$1.80$$
$$= \$16.75$$

STEP 5:

Present value the aggregate fair stake at the one-year riskless interest rate of 8% p.a. to arrive at the fair present value of the call option:

$$\text{fair call option price} = \frac{\$16.75}{(1.08)^1}$$

$$= \$15.51$$

CONCLUSION

The Do-It-Yourself option pricing model embodies most of what is important in connection with an understanding of option pricing. Those advantages which more complex mod-

Figure 8–3

Future Price	Probability	Payoff	Fair Stake
$65	1%	$0	$0
$75	4%	$0	$0
$85	10%	$0	$0
$95	20%	$5	$1
$105	27%	$15	$4.05
$115	20%	$25	$5
$125	14%	$35	$4.90
$135	4%	$45	$1.80

els enjoy over the Do-It-Yourself model derive from the fact that they—the more complex models—(i) combine our five analytical steps into one formula and (ii) embody mechanisms by which possible future prices of the underlying commodity and their attendant probabilities are derived. But we will see that while such mechanisms, which comprise statistical techniques by which past price behavior is used as a predictor of the future, may relieve us of a good deal of burdensome independent analysis, they do not necessarily make our results any more accurate, valid, or sound.

Chapter 9

9

An Introduction to Options

BASIC TERMINOLOGY

Conventional options confer on the holder the right either (i) in the case of *call* options, to *buy*, or (ii) in the case of *put* options, to *sell*, a specified commodity at a specified price on, or before, a specified date. A call option we will refer to simply as a "call." A put option we will refer to simply as a "put."

A particular option's essential characteristics, of which its value will be a function, are:

- the *underlying commodity*—i.e., the thing, and how much of it, which the option confers the right to buy or sell;

- the price (the *exercise price*, or *strike price*) at which the underlying commodity may be bought or sold by way of the option; and

- the time during which, or at which, the option confers the right to buy or sell the commodity. Some options allow the holder to exercise the right to buy or sell the underlying commodity at any time up to the date on which the option expires (the *expiration date*). Because such options are more common in the American markets than elsewhere, they are termed *American* options. Where the terms of an option provide only for the holder to exercise the option on one specific date (the expiration date being the only, and thus the last, date for exercise), the option is termed a *European* option.

As the analysis of option pricing is evolved, it will be convenient to denote each of the essential characteristics of an option with a short-form notation:

- the current or spot value of the underlying commodity (i.e., that prevailing at the time the analysis is being performed) will be denoted by 'S';

- the exercise price of the option will be denoted by 'E'; and

- the period to expiration (or simply the "expiration") of the option will be expressed as we expressed the period to a delivery date in our analysis of forward and futures pricing—that is, in terms of n compounding periods. Again, as in the forward and futures pricing analyses, 'n' will be assumed to express years, unless otherwise stated.

Further

- the fair value of a call option will be denoted by 'C', and the fair value of a put option will be denoted by 'P'.

A NOTE ON OPTIONS MARKETS

Before moving on, it is as well to distinguish between various senses of the word "option." As we have defined them, "options" include all financial instruments which confer the right, but not the obligation, to buy or to sell a specified commodity at a specified price during, or at, a specified time. Under this broad definition are subsumed both the options contracts which are traded on the major stock, commodity and options exchanges of the world and those which are created and sold off of the exchanges.

As with futures contracts, exchange-traded options are highly standardized. In the case of U.S. stock options, the underlying commodity is invariably a lot of 100 shares. Performance is underpinned by the exchange's clearing house.[1] Exchange-traded contracts are in most cases liquid

---

[1] Note that option sellers (or "writers") must deposit cash or securities as margin against their liability to the clearing house. Margin requirements vary from time to time and from broker to broker, so it is to the relevant exchange or to your broker that you should go for more information on these matters.

and they are often—as we shall see—used in hedging and arbitrage strategies involving positions in the underlying commodity. In most cases they have initial expirations which are less than one year.

Over-the-counter options differ from exchange-traded options in much the same way as forward contracts differ from futures contracts. The over-the-counter instruments are "options" in the broad sense, but are often highly illiquid. As such, they are often used as investment vehicles—surrogates for the underlying commodity—rather than as hedging or arbitrage vehicles. They often have long initial expirations—up to seven years or more—and since (as we shall see) expiration is positively correlated with an option's (broad sense) value, they are most often significantly more expensive than exchange-traded options.

These differences and others will be discussed at greater length in the following chapter, when we come to deal with warrants. Until that point, however, it is as well to remember that while traders and stockbrokers often use the word "option" to signify an exchange-traded option, almost all that will be said in this and coming chapters about option-pricing theory applies to options in the broad sense. Where pricing, rather than pricing theory, is concerned, however, it will also help to bear in mind that exchange-traded options markets are typically more efficient than the off-exchange markets, implying that actual prices on these markets will correlate more closely with those implied by our theoretical models.

INTRINSIC VALUE

In the case of a call option, if S exceeds E the call is said to be "in-the-money." A holder of such a call could take an amount E, and use it to exercise the option, receiving a commodity worth S. His effective profit would thus be $S - E$. This is termed the *intrinsic value* of the call.

Conversely, a call option for which E exceeds S is said to be "*out-of-the-money.*" It will never be worthwhile to exercise an out-of-the-money call, for it means paying the exercise price in order to buy something which can be more cheaply purchased in the spot market. An out-of-the-money option thus has no intrinsic value.

A put, which allows the holder to sell for E a commodity with a then market value of S, is in-the-money if E exceeds S. The holder's effective profit upon exercise would be $E - S$, which is the put's intrinsic value. When $E < S$ then a put is out-of-the-money and has no intrinsic value.

When S and E are equal an option, whether a call or a put, is said to be "at-the-money." An at-the-money option has no intrinsic value, because there is no effective profit or loss to be had from its immediate exercise.

THE PAYOFF OF AN OPTION

The *payoff* from an option at the time of its exercise or expiration is the option's intrinsic value at that time. Let us signify the spot market value of an underlying commodity at the time of exercise or expiration of an option by 'S_e'. The payoff of a call will be $S_e - E$ in the event that $S_e > E$ (i.e., if the call is in-the-money), and zero if the call is out-of- or at-the-money. It will, in other words, be the higher of $S_e - E$ and zero. We will signify this payoff by '$max(S_e - E, 0)$'.

The payoff analysis for put options is just the opposite of that for calls. A put's intrinsic value at any point in time is the higher of $E - S_e$ and zero. The payoff of a put—its intrinsic value at the time of exercise or expiration—is therefore $max(E - S_e, 0)$.

We can graph the payoff of an option as a function of the spot market price of the underlying commodity at the time of the option's exercise. For a call, the payoff will obviously increase as the spot price of the underlying commodity increases above the exercise price—that is, $max(S_e - E, 0)$ will increase as S_e increases above E. Conversely, the payoff of a put will decrease with an increase in the spot price of the underlying commodity, until the spot price reaches the exercise price of the put, after which it will be zero. The payoffs of a long call position and of a long put position as a function of the price of the underlying commodity are described in Figures 9–1 and 9–2.

An investor who sells an option is said to have "*written*" the option. The seller is thus often termed the "writer" of the option. The payoff associated with a short call position and a short put position can also be graphed. The short position payoff is simply the mirror image about the *x*-axis of the payoff of the corresponding long option position, as set forth in Figures 9–3 and 9–4.

TIME VALUE

Even though an option is out-of-the-money it is not necessarily worthless, for there is some probability of S rising or falling before its expiration so that the option *comes to have* intrinsic value, and thus to afford a payoff. The option will be worth something to the extent that such a probability exists. And such a probability (however small) will normally exist so long as the option is 'live'—that is, so long as the option has some time remaining before expiration (i.e., so long as $n > 0$). It is for this reason—the potential to become more intrinsically valuable tomorrow than it is today—that any option will normally be valued above its intrinsic value. An option's market price less its intrinsic value—that portion

Figure 9–1

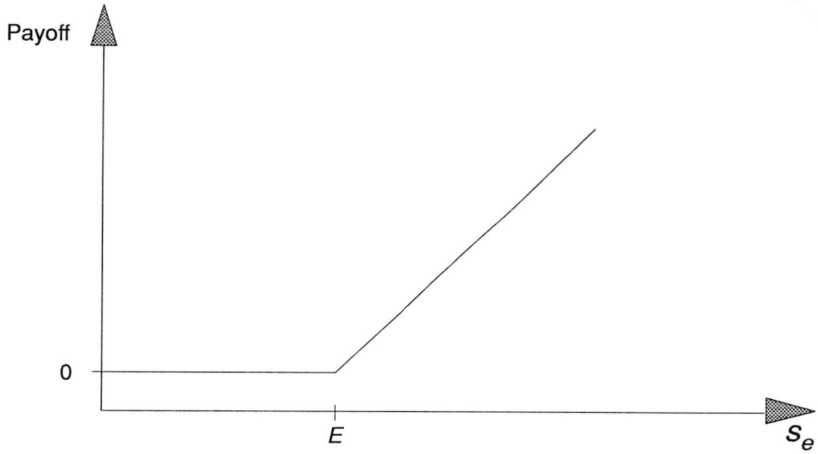

Figure 9–2

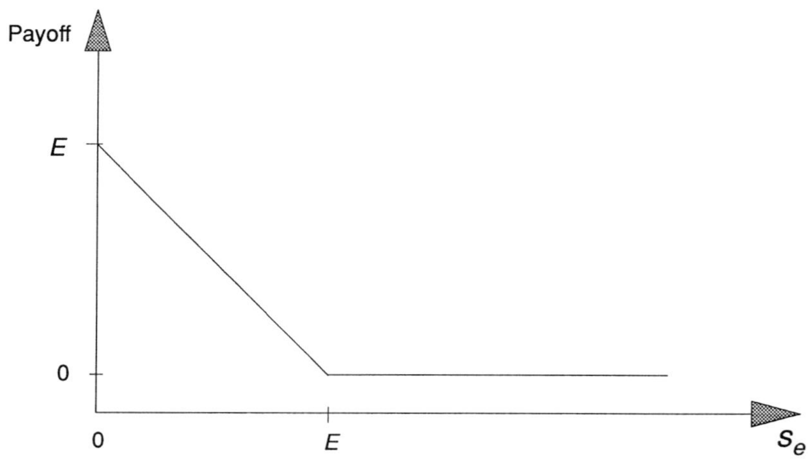

Figure 9–3

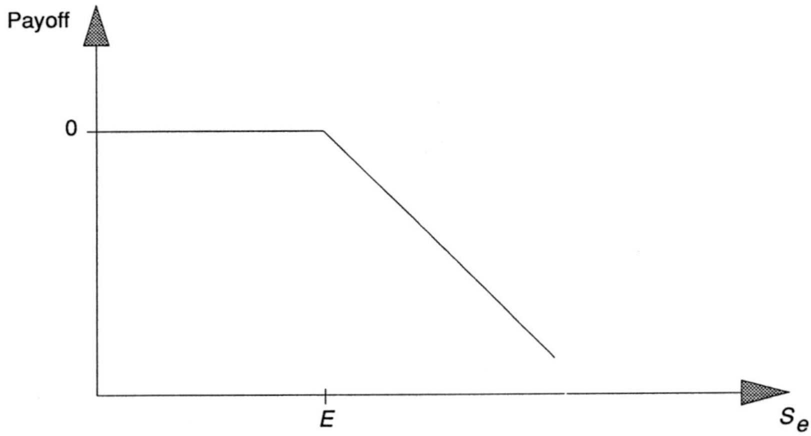

Figure 9–4

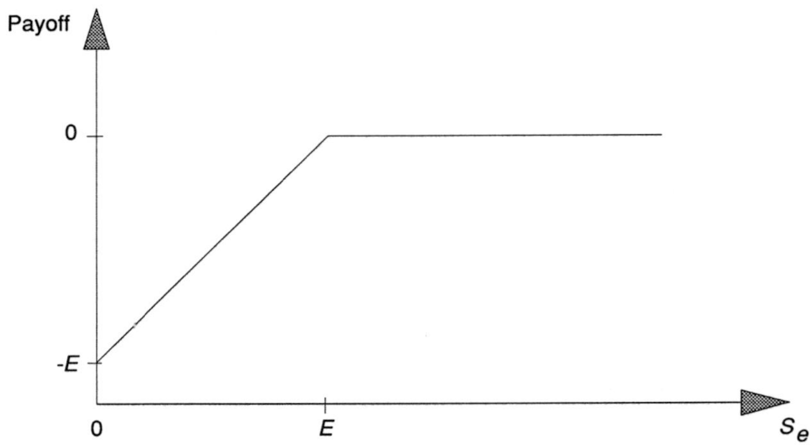

of the option's price which reflects this potential for appreciation—is often termed its *"time value."*

SOME BASIC RELATIONSHIPS

The Relationship between C and n and between P and n

The above description of time value brings us to the relationship between the value of an option and n. So long as n exceeds zero—so long as the option remains unexpired—there will normally be some chance, some probability, that S will be higher by the time $n = 0$ than it is today. Thus, if an investor has the choice between two call options, identical in every respect except for n, he will choose the option where n is the greatest. As the other option expires his will still be 'live', conferring a probability—however slight—of a greater payoff. His preference will be reflected in the higher value he ascribes to the option with the greatest n.

Thus, in the case of a call option, as all else remains equal, C increases as n increases. Similarly, among two put options, identical in all respects other than n, the highest value will be accorded to the put with the greatest n, since this option will still be 'live' as the other expires. Hence, for puts also, P increases as n increases.

The Relationship between C and S and between P and S

Suppose the stock of ABC Corporation is currently trading at \$100 per share (i.e., S = \$100). If a call option into one share is available with an exercise price (E) of \$80, then the value of the call option, C, must be at least equal to the option's intrinsic value of \$20. Any lower price would give rise to an obvious arbitrage opportunity, allowing for an investor to buy the call (cost: C), exercise it (assuming it to be an American call) for \$80, and find himself in possession of a share valued at \$100. The arbitrage profit would be the \$100 share value less the aggregate cost of purchasing the option and exercising it. In other words,

$$C \geq S - E \text{, or}$$

$$C + E \geq S$$

Thus in the case of a call option, with all else being equal, the higher *S*, the higher *C*.

For a put option, the opposite applies:

$$P \geq E - S \text{, or}$$

$$E - P \geq S$$

All else being equal, in other words, the value of the put, *P*, declines as *S* increases.

The Relationship between C and E and between P and E

In the same manner, it is more attractive to hold a call option exercisable at a lower exercise price than one exercisable at a higher exercise price. In other words, with all else remaining equal, *C* rises as *E* falls. For a put option, with all else being equal, *P* falls as *E* falls, since it is less attractive to have the right to sell a commodity at a lower price than at a higher price.

THE USE OF OPTIONS: HEDGERS AND SPECULATORS

As will be shown in the coming section, options represent a means by which investors can transfer certain types of risk associated with a particular investment. They cannot entirely eliminate such risk from the marketplace as a whole. Investors who use options in conjunction with cash, forward, or futures positions in order to reduce their exposure to potential losses stemming from price fluctuations in the underlying commodity are termed "*hedgers.*" Investors who use options in order to add to their exposure to the underlying commodity are termed "*speculators.*"

For the hedger, the crucial feature of all options, whether calls or puts, is that they can afford "downside protection" against losses arising from a fall in the price of the underlying commodity. This is obviously true of puts, which allow the holder to sell the underlying commodity at the pre-determined exercise price, and thus confer a floor price for the holder of that commodity. It is, however, an often-missed truth also about calls.

A call option confers downside protection because it confers 'control' over a large volume of the underlying commodity for a relatively small outlay. Holding, say, an at-the-money call option means that if the price of the commodity falls over the call's life then the call will be thrown away unexercised. The call holder's total loss will be, at most, the cost of the call. Buying the underlying commodity, however, exposes the investor to a potential loss equal to the cost of that commodity. Since a call option will always be priced lower, and most often significantly lower, than the cost of the underlying commodity, a call option holder's maximum downside risk—loss of his whole investment—will be less than that of an investor in the underlying commodity itself.

We can express this downside protection feature of call options by tabulating the costs and benefits of owning the underlying commodity against those of owning a call, as in Figure 9–5. The total profit associated with the purchase of the underlying commodity is $S_e - S$, while that associated with the call is $max(S_e - E, 0) - C$. Suppose that the cost of the

Figure 9–5

	Underlying Commodity	Call Option
Initial Investment	S	C
Payoff	S_e	$max(S_e - E, 0)$

option—C—is just 20% of the cost of the underlying commodity (i.e., $C = 0.2S$). Now look what happens if the underlying commodity falls substantially in price, say to half its initial cost (i.e., $S_e = 0.5S$). The profit associated with the underlying commodity is then a negative—a loss of—$0.5S$. That associated with the call, however, is only a negative $0.2S$.

But what happens if the underlying commodity rises in value, suppose, to double its initial cost? In this case the profit from the underlying commodity will be S. The profit from the call, meanwhile, will be $max(2S - E, 0) - 0.2S$. The profit from the underlying commodity, in other words, will exceed the profit from the call so long as $E > 0.8S$.

Typically, a call will confer a smaller profit than a purchase of the underlying commodity when the commodity rises substantially in price, but as the *quid pro quo*, a call will result in a smaller loss than the underlying commodity in the event the commodity falls substantially in price. This is the sense in which calls confer downside protection, and it is a feature we examine in more detail below. But it should be noted here that this feature appears to many people to be counter-intuitive—particularly because it suggests calls may be somewhat conservative investments, whereas most people tend to think of options as highly speculative. This apparent paradox will be cleared up by the analysis of the following sections.

DEFINING THE MINIMUM VALUE OF A CALL

Suppose you have $100 to invest in ABC Corporation, which is still trading at $100 per share. Each ABC common share pays a $5 dividend annually, and ABC has announced its intention to maintain a $5 dividend for the coming year. There is a call option which is exercisable into one share of ABC common stock after one year ($n = 1$) at an exercise price of $90.

If you buy the ABC share, one year hence you will find yourself in possession of a $5 dividend plus the share, the then current market value of which—call it S_e—is unknown at present. Your cash flows would thus be as set forth in Figure 9–6.

Consider how the cash flow of $\$5 + S_e$ one year hence can be replicated with a deposit and by using the ABC call option *as though it were a forward contract* (as though, in other words,

Figure 9–6

Year	Cash Flow
0	<$100>
1	$\$5 + S_e$

the option conferred the *obligation* to purchase the ABC share, rather than the *right* to do so). This entails depositing the present value of the $5 dividend plus the option's $90 exercise price and then using $90 of the maturing deposit to exercise the call, whether the prevailing price of an ABC share is higher or lower than the $90 exercise price.

The discount rate to use for the purpose of computing the PV of the dividend should embody the same degree of risk as that associated with the payment of the dividend. It will, as discussed in earlier chapters, thus usually be higher than the riskless rate. If the appropriate "risky" one-year rate is 8% p.a., then

$$PV(\$5) = \frac{\$5}{(1.08)^1} = \$4.72$$

To compute the PV of the option's $90 exercise price, the discount rate to use is the riskless rate; we must be sure of having the $90 available to exercise the option. The amount we need to deposit at the one-year riskless interest rate of, say, 6% p.a., in order to receive repayment of $90 of interest and principal after one year, is $\$90/(1.06)^1$, or $84.91.

If we (i) buy the call on one share of ABC stock (cost: *C*), and (ii) simultaneously invest an aggregate of $89.63 for one year ($84.91 at the riskless deposit rate of 6% p.a., and $4.72 at the risky deposit rate of 8% p.a.), and then (iii) exercise the option one year hence, using the $90 from the maturing 6% p.a. deposit, we will have replicated exactly the risk profile and the one-year cash flow associated with holding one ABC share. That is, we will receive $95 from our maturing deposits, of which we will apply $90 to the exercise of the option, leaving us with $5 replicating the dividend. We will also be left in possession of one ABC share with a then current market value of S_e. The comparative cash flows are set out in Figure 9–7.

As we saw in earlier chapters, if two portfolios afford the same payoff under all circumstances (as do the above portfolios of the ABC share, on the one hand, and the exercised option plus the deposits, on the other) then they must cost the same. Any difference in cost would give rise to an arbitrage opportunity. We can thus derive the no-arbitrage value of C:

$$\$100 = C + \$84.91 + \$4.72$$

$$C = \$10.37$$

This analysis, however, supposes that there is no alternative to exercising the option. Of course, an 'option' which conferred no alternative to exercise would really be a forward position in the underlying commodity. But options differ from forward and futures contracts exactly insofar as there *is* an alternative to exercising them. And sometimes it will be economically advantageous to pursue this alternative—viz, when an option is out-of-the-money.

Figure 9–7

	Cash Flows				
Year	**Buy Share Spot**	=	**Buy and Exercise Call Option**	+	**Make Deposit of \$84.91 plus \$4.72**
0	<\$100>		<C>		<\$84.91>+ <\$4.72>
1	\$5 + S_e		<\$90> + S_e		\$90 + \$5

Suppose, for example, that the ABC share falls by $15 during the coming year, so that S_e = $85. Now consider the cash flows associated with the portfolios comprising the ABC share on the one hand and the call option plus the two deposits on the other. If the option is not exercised at expiration, the payoff of the latter portfolio is significantly higher than that of the former (see Figure 9–8).

Using Figure 9–7, it can be shown that the holder of the portfolio comprising the option plus deposits, if he exercises the option, will receive the same cash flow and thus be equally well-off as the holder of the ABC share. Now it has been shown that if he rationally lets the option lapse unexercised, he will enjoy a higher one-year cash flow, and will thus be better-off than the holder of the ABC share. If the holder of the portfolio comprising the option and the deposits is at least as well-off as, and under certain circumstances better-off

Figure 9–8

	Cash Flows		
Year	**Buy Share Spot**	**Buy Call Option and Let Lapse**	**+ Make Deposit of $84.91 plus $4.72**
0	<$100>	<C>	<$84.91> + <$4.72>
1	$5 + $85		$90 + $5

than, the holder of the ABC share, then his portfolio must be at least as valuable as the ABC share. In other words,

$$C + \$84.91 + \$4.72 \geq \$100$$

from which

$$C_{min} = \$10.37$$

This minimum value is derived on the basis that a call option must be at least as valuable as a forward contract. For a call option allows the holder to do what a forward contract obliges the holder to do, but the option also allows the holder the alternative to do something a forward contract does not—viz, throw the option away unexercised in the event the value of the underlying commodity is low. In the above equation, remember, \$100 is the current value of the ABC share (*S*), \$84.91 is the PV of the option's exercise price (i.e., *PV(E)*), and \$4.72 is the PV of the income accruing on the ABC share up to expiration of the option (i.e., *PV(div)*). Thus,

$$C_{min} = S - PV(E) - PV(div)$$

This is no more than a slightly different form of the forward and futures pricing equation, Equation 3(1a), as it was evolved in Chapter 3. It says that the minimum value of a call is its value as a forward, or futures, contract. But unlike a forward or futures contract, an option can never be worth less than nothing—it will not be exercised in the event that its intrinsic value is negative. Taking this refinement into consideration, we can express this conclusion as follows: the minimum value of a call option is equal to the spot price of the underlying commodity, less the PV of the option's exercise price (discounted at the riskless interest rate), less the PV of the income accruing on the underlying commodity up to the option's expiration (discounted at a rate which reflects the risk associated with such income), subject to a minimum of zero.

It is often taken for granted that the higher of zero and an option's intrinsic value (the higher of $S - E$ and 0 for a call, $E - S$ and 0 in the case of a put) defines the minimum value of that option. However, our above analysis shows that the minimum value of a call option (C_{min}) will actually *exceed* $S - E$ when

$$PV(E) + PV(div) < E$$

In connection with calls on non-income bearing commodities, such as precious metals, $PV(div)$ is zero; therefore, the minimum value of the call will *always* be greater than its intrinsic value, *so long as discount rates are greater than zero.* Since, upon exercise of a call option, the investor's payoff is its then intrinsic value of $S - E$, it will never be rational to exercise such a call option prior to its expiration. To do so would be to receive a payoff which is less than the call's minimum value.

How is this conclusion to be intuitively explained? The answer is simple. When we deal with a European-type call option, the underlying commodity is really a forward position, rather than a cash position in the commodity. When we buy such a European call, it is impossible to take delivery of the commodity prior to the option's expiration, in the same way that with a forward contract it is impossible to take delivery of the underlying commodity prior to the delivery date. Since we have shown that, with respect to calls on non-income bearing commodities, it can never be advantageous to exercise the call prior to its expiration, the same applies—it may not be 'physically' impossible to exercise such a call early, but it is 'economically' unreasonble to do so.

However, the call option confers downside protection which a forward contract does not, and it is this downside protection feature—the ability to throw the call away unexercised in the event the price of the underlying commodity is low—that accounts for the excess of a call option's actual price (*C*) over its value as a forward contract. In other words,

$$C = S - PV(E) - PV(div) + \textit{value of downside protection feature}$$

RELATING THE PRICE OF EUROPEAN PUTS AND CALLS: PUT-CALL PARITY

Before progressing to an analysis of the value of the downside protection feature conferred by options, we should consider the relationship between the value of a call and that of a put. There is a natural temptation to think of puts and calls as different types of animals. We have already touched upon the temptation to focus on puts as conferring protection against a fall in the price of the underlying commodity, and on calls as being essentially speculative investments which confer a benefit in the event of a rise in the price of the underlying commodity. That myth should now have been laid to rest. But if the value of both puts and calls lies in the downside protection they confer, how are those values related? Again, the answer is simple.

Consider how owning a portfolio comprising a one-year European call with an exercise price of *E* will have an identical payoff to a portfolio comprising a one-year forward contract with a forward price of *E*, along with a one-year European put with an exercise price of *E*. If the price of the commodity rises during the year, the holder of the call would exercise it (cost of exercise: *E*) and would be left in possession of the commodity (then current value: S_e). The owner of the long forward plus put portfolio, meanwhile, will buy the commodity on the delivery date (forward price: *E*) and will throw away the put unexercised. He, too, will be left in possession of the commodity, the then current value of which is S_e.

Conversely, if the price of the commodity drops during the year, the holder of the call will throw it away unexercised and will be left holding nothing. The holder of the long forward plus put portfolio, meanwhile, will—as he is obliged to do—buy the commodity pursuant to the forward contract (cost: *E*) and will immediately resell it pursuant to the exercise of the put for a price of *E* (i.e., the exercise price of the put). Again, like the holder of the call, this portfolio holder's net position will be nothing. Hence, the payoff of the call portfolio is, under all circumstances, identical to that of the put plus long forward portfolio. There is said to be "parity" between them (Figure 9–9).

Yet again, we can invoke an arbitrage pricing rationale, and point out that if two portfolios afford the same payoff under all circumstances (as do the two portfolios above) then they will cost the same, or an arbitrage opportunity will exist. Using this equality we can relate *C* and *P*:

$$C = P + c$$

where

> *C* is the price of a European call, with an exercise price of *E* and an expiration of *n* years;
>
> *P* is the price of a European put, with an exercise price of *E* and expiration of *n* years; and
>
> *c* is the present value of a forward contract conferring the obligation to purchase the underlying commodity after *n* years at a forward price of *E*.

Figure 9–9

If S_e Turns Out to Be:	Portfolio of One Call (Cost: C)	Portfolio of Put Plus Forward Contract (Cost: $P + c$)
Less than or equal to E	Call not exercised Payoff = \$0	Future settled—E paid and commodity received. Put exercised —E received and commodity delivered Net Payoff = \$0
Greater than E	Call exercised—E paid and commodity received Net payoff = $S_e - E$	Future settled—E paid and commodity received. Put unexercised Net payoff = $S_e - E$

We can now use the expanded general forward and futures pricing (Equation 4(1)), developed in Chapter 4, to substitute for c:

$$C = P + S - \sum_{j=1}^{n} \frac{CF_j}{(1+R)^j} - \frac{E}{(1+r)^n}$$

where

C and P have the meanings ascribed above;

S is the spot price of the underlying commodity;

n is the number of compounding periods up to the expiration of both the put and call;

CF_j is the cash flow associated with the underlying commodity in the jth compounding period;

R is the risky interest or discount rate per compounding period, by which it is appropriate to present value the cash flows associated with the underlying commodity;

E is the exercise price of both the put and the call; and

r is the riskless interest or discount rate per compounding period.

The verbal expression of the whole equation reads:

> The value of a European call is equal to (i) that of a European put (same underlying commodity, same exercise price and same expiration), plus (ii) the spot price of the underlying commodity, less (iii) the PV of the income accruing on the commodity up to the option's expiration (discounted at the appropriate risky rate), less (iv) the PV of the option's exercise price, discounted at the riskless rate.

We can use the short-form notation developed during the earlier examination of discounted cash flow analysis to express this concisely:

$$C = P + S - PV(\textit{income accruing on underlying commodity}) - PV(E)$$

A NOTE ON AMERICAN VERSUS EUROPEAN OPTIONS

In this background analysis of options we have either dealt with European-type options (those that can be exercised only at their expiration) or have neglected the possibility of early exercise of an option. Indeed, the discussion of the minimum value of a call illustrates that it will never be rational to exercise a call on a non-income bearing commodity prior to its expiration. But what about American options, which can be exercised at any time during their life into income-bearing commodities? Surely, since such options can be exercised at expiration they must be at least as valuable as European options. Moreover, since they confer the additional opportunity to exercise before expiration, is it not true that they may be more valuable than European options?

In the remainder of this chapter, we will examine the following important questions: what are the principles at play in determining the optimal timing of an option's exercise; and what is the value attributable to the opportunity to exercise an option before its expiration?

Calls on Non-Income Bearing Commodities

At the time a call option is exercised, the holder pays the exercise price—E—and receives the underlying commodity which at the point of exercise is worth, say, \$100. His payoff is thus $\$100 - E$, the option's intrinsic value. We have already determined, however, that the minimum value of a call on a non-income bearing commodity will always be higher than its intrinsic value, so long as discount rates exceed zero (if rates are—inconceivably—zero, then the minimum value of such a call will equal its intrinsic value). If the profit or payoff to be realized by exercising the option is its intrinsic value, and the value of the unexercised option exceeds this amount, clearly it is not rational to opt to exercise prior to expiration.

Since it will always be economically disadvantageous to exercise a call option on a non-income bearing commodity before its expiration, the value of a European call on such a commodity will always equal that of an American call.

Calls on Income-Bearing Commodities

Under what circumstances, if any, can it be economically advantageous to exercise a call on an income-bearing commodity prior to its expiration? A rational investor will want to exercise an option, rather than leave it unexercised, when the income to be earned by owning the commodity itself is sufficiently large. Suppose you own an American call option, exercisable into one share of ABC common stock at E per share. The expiration of the option is one year.

If you exercise the call today your payoff will be the current spot market value of the share received ($S_{current}$), less the exercise price of E. With the share, of course, you also gain entitlement to any income accruing on it in the future. Suppose the prospective dividend is \$8 per share, payable one year hence. Discounted at the rate, R, which reflects the risk associated with it, the coming year's dividend has a present value of $\$8/(1+R)^1$. The present value of the payoff plus income to be realized by exercising the call today will thus be $S_{current} - E + \$8/(1+R)^1$.

If, on the other hand, you defer and exercise the call at its expiration, what will happen? You will, at expiration, receive the underlying ABC share (the present value of which is $S_{current}$) and you will pay the exercise price of E, the present value of which is $E/(1+r)^1$. The present value of the payoff to be realized by exercising the call one year hence, at its expiration, will thus be $S_{current} - E/(1{+}r)^1$. This is the only payoff, of course, that a European call option is capable of conferring if exercised, since such a call is not capable of being exercised early.

Now, it is clear that the value of an American call option may exceed that of an otherwise identical European call option when the payoff to be realized from an immediate exercise exceeds that (expressed in present value terms) to be realized by deferring exercise until the expiration of the option. That is, in our example, when

$$S_{current} - E + \frac{8}{(1{+}R)^1} > S_{current} - \frac{E}{(1{+}r)^1}$$

Expressed in general terms:

$C_{American}$ may exceed $C_{European}$ if

$$\frac{E}{(1{+}r)^n} + \sum_{j=1}^{n} \frac{CF_j}{(1{+}R)^j} > E$$

That is, if

PV(E) + PV(income accruing on underlying commodity) > E

This condition, again, cannot obtain for calls on non-income bearing commodities (that is, where $CF_j = 0$), and cannot even represent an equality so long as $r > 0$.

At this point, this is as much as needs to be said about the relationship between American and European calls. A brief analysis of the relationship between American and European puts is all that is required to complete preliminary discussion of the two types of options and the value of early exercise.

Puts on Income and Non-Income Bearing Commodities

The holder of a put option who exercises that option prior to its expiration receives the exercise price (E) and, in return, delivers the underlying commodity, the current value of which we will again call $S_{current}$. His payoff on exercise is thus $E - S_{current}$.

The holder who defers exercise of a put to its expiration, on the other hand, retains entitlement to the income accruing on the underlying commodity. This holder, too, ultimately delivers the underlying commodity (current value: $S_{current}$), but he does not receive the exercise price until he exercises the option. In present value terms, the exercise price which is to be received in n years is thus worth $E/(1+r)^n$ today. Substituting 'S' for '$S_{current}$', we can express the deferring holder's payoff from the put in PV terms:

$$\sum_{j=1}^{n} \frac{CF_j}{(1+R)^j} - S + \frac{E}{(1+r)^n}$$

If the income to be realized by exercising a put today exceeds that to be realized by deferring exercise until expiration, then the value of an American-type put option, which permits such early exercise, may exceed that of an otherwise identical European put option, which does not. An American put may thus be more valuable than a European put when

$$E - S > \sum_{j=1}^{n} \frac{CF_j}{(1+R)^j} - S + \frac{E}{(1+r)^n}$$

Now, this condition may obtain even for puts on non-income bearing commodities. That is, though $CF_j = 0$, E still may exceed $E/(1+r)^n$. Indeed, E will exceed $E/(1+r)^n$ so long as r is greater than zero. Hence, an American put may be more valuable than a European put, whether the underlying commodity is income-bearing or not.

We have shown that it will never be economically advantageous to exercise calls on non-income bearing commodities prior to their expiration by showing that C_{min} is never less than the intrinsic value of the option, and we have shown that, in respect of puts on non-income bearing commodities, there may be conditions under which early exercise is warranted. When dealing with options on income-bearing commodities, there may be some advantage (and thus some value) to owning American-type puts and calls, rather than European-type puts and calls. The possibility that conditions favoring early exercise may obtain enhances the value of the American options relative to their European cousins.

A detailed analysis of the differential in values between American and European-type options is beyond the scope of this chapter—indeed, of this book. Bear in mind, however, that the concept of probability is once again key. The additional value of an American option over a European option will increase as the probability of one of the conditions obtaining for early exercise increases.

A FINAL NOTE ON MINIMUM OPTION VALUES AND PUT-CALL PARITY

The equations derived in this chapter concerning the minimum value of European call, European put-call parity and American-European option values may appear complicated at first sight. Do not, however, be put-off by appearances. It is not necessary for anyone—not even specialist option traders—to learn these formulae. Most members of the financial community will never be required to apply them in real-life problems. What you do need to take away from the foregoing analyses, however, are:

- an understanding of a call option as embodying downside protection against a fall in the price of the underlying commodity;

- an understanding that what underlies a European option is a forward position in a commodity rather than a cash position. The real intrinsic value (and thus the real minimum value) of such a call is $f - E$, where f is the break-even forward price of the underlying commodity rather than $S - E$; and

- an understanding that a European call can be replicated using a portfolio comprising a forward position (forward price of E and delivery n periods hence) in the underlying commodity plus a European put (same E, same n).

Once this conceptual framework is established, the minimum European call price equation and the European put-call parity equation can be readily derived by applying the basic mathematics of discounted cash flow analysis.

Chapter 10

10

Warrants

ALL WARRANTS ARE OPTIONS

In the opening paragraph of Chapter 9, an option was described as an instrument conferring on the holder the right to buy (in the case of a call), or to sell (in the case of a put) a specified commodity at a specified price on, or before, a specified date. If this is a working *definition* of an option then a warrant is an option, for a warrant confers upon the holder exactly this kind of a right. Warrants come in both call and put forms, but put forms are somewhat rare and found mostly where the underlying commodity is a currency or stock index.

While, by the description of Chapter 9, warrants *are* options, we must be careful to distinguish between the word "option" as it is used to denote a broad class of instruments, included among which are warrants, and the word "option" as it is often used by traders and stockbrokers, to denote a much narrower range of short term exchange-traded contracts (see "A Note on Options Markets" in Chapter 9). Almost all that has been said concerning option valuation and pricing applies to "options" in the broad sense and thus to warrants. But it is as well to add a few remarks in this chapter concerning the features which distinguish warrants from options in the narrow sense.

Warrants are issued by and represent obligations of—typically—some corporate entity. Warrants which are exercisable into shares of common stock (innovatively termed "stock warrants") are often issued along with bonds or new shares of stock, as a sort of 'kicker' or inducement to investors.[1] Payment of the exercise price must normally be made in cash, although in some cases—of which more will be said in the following chapter on convertible bonds—the exercise price can be satisfied by surrender of some other commodity, such as the bond to which the warrant originally comes attached. The shares that become deliverable upon exercise of the warrant—or the bonds which become deliverable upon exercise of a bond warrant—will often be new securities, held in reserve by the warrant issuer.

That their exercise is typically a *dilutive event* which increases the amount of the underlying commodity in circulation[2] is the only feature which requires us to modify option

---

[1] The use of warrants as 'kickers' is consistent with all that has so far been said about options in the broad sense and with all that we know about investor psychology. For one thing, an issue of warrants alone would be singularly unappealing to a corporation as a funding mechanism since the amounts raised up-front from the sale of the warrants would be small relative to, say, the amounts realized when and if the warrants are exercised. At the same time warrants are, as implied by the gambling metaphor invoked in our earlier analysis, speculative instruments. So far as the investor is concerned they are, for this reason, typically unattractive as core investments. Nevertheless they are often attractive as part of a package, where their cost can easily be 'lost' among the other elements of the package.

[2] It is not always the case, however, that the exercise of even stock warrants will constitute a dilutive event. Warrants may occasionally be issued by one entity and be exercisable into the stock of a third party. Because the issuer of such warrants will typically have hedged

(narrow sense) pricing theory for warrants. For the value of an option (broad sense, including warrants) is a function of the value of the underlying commodity, but the value of the underlying commodity is itself typically a function of the amount of the commodity in circulation. The value of a share of stock, for example, will decrease as the number of shares outstanding increases, since the company's value has to be divided among the higher number of claims.[3] As a general rule, the greater the "dilutive overhang" represented by the warrants, and the greater the "discount" at which the warrants confer the right to buy the underlying commodity, the greater the corrosive effect of the exercise or potential exercise of those warrants on the value of the stock. A simple example should serve to illustrate the relationship.

Suppose that Global Bi-Widget Corporation, a small company with big ambitions, currently has 100 common shares outstanding. These shares are trading at $20 each. GB-W now issues 100 warrants at a price of $2 per warrant. Each warrant confers the right to purchase one share at an exercise price of $10. Were all the warrants to be exercised immediately there would be 200 GB-W shares in issue. The value of GB-W to its shareholders has, of course, increased only by the $1,200 which the company realizes from the sale and exercise of the warrants. To the extent its value to shareholders prior to the issuance of the warrants was $2,000 (that is, the 100 shares in issue at the time multiplied by the $20 per share price), its value post the issuance and exercise is $3,200. This value is now allocated among the 200 shares in issue, giving each

---

the sale with a long position in the underlying stock, such issues are often termed "covered warrants" issues. Covered warrants of this sort are amenable to exactly the same valuation approach as options in the narrow sense.

[3] The same generally applies where bonds are the underlying commodity. Their value is also a function of the number in issue. For one thing, a company will often stand more chance of defaulting on payments due in respect of, say, $100 million of bonds than it will in respect of $50 million of bonds. Against this, however, must be weighed the value to the investor of the enhanced liquidity typically associated with a larger issue.

share a value of $16, i.e., $4 lower than the share value prior to the issuance. The warrants, while they appeared at first sight to be $10 in-the-money, now appear to be just $4 in-the-money at issuance. Had the warrants been exercisable at $16 per share, on the other hand, the corrosive effect would have been substantially less—the equity value of GB-W post the issuance and exercise of the warrants would be $3,800, and the value of each share would thus be $19.

Contrast this with the situation in which 100 exchange-traded GB-W options are issued, exercisable at $10 per share. These options do not, as they are exercised, result in the issuance of new shares, their exercise merely entails the transfer of shares from one person to another. Since none of the exercise price paid upon exercise of an option finds its way to the company, the company's equity value—its value to shareholders—is unaffected by the issuance or exercise of the options. The common stock of the company (barring any other change in its business outlook or in market conditions) continues to be worth $2,000, and this value continues to be allocated among 100 shares. There is no corrosive effect on the stock price and the options truly are $10 in-the-money at issuance.

ADJUSTING FOR DILUTION[4]

An approximate adjustment to take account of the corrosive effect of dilution on the value of a common stock (or the

[4] The terms of most issues of warrants and convertible debentures provide for the adjustment of the exercise or conversion price upon the issuance of shares of stock or other securities (including further issuances of warrants and convertible debentures) to compensate for the corrosive effects of such issuances on their conversion value. Such provisions are termed "antidilution provisions" and form an important part of a warrant or convertible debenture prospectus.

corrosive effect of potential dilution, because the issuance of dilutive instruments will often drive down stock values *in anticipation* of eventual dilution) can be factored into the Do-It-Yourself model.[5] From the GB-W example it can be seen that:

> *equity value of the firm after warrant exercise (call it V_2) = equity value before exercise (V_1) + aggregate exercise price received.*

Since the aggregate exercise price is equal to the product of the number of warrants exercised (call it W) and the exercise price per warrant (call it E_1), we have

$$V_2 = V_1 + (W \times E_1)$$

This analysis assumes, however, that the stock of the firm is non-dividend paying, since an increase in the amount of dividend paying stock in circulation would place an incremental dividend burden on the company. We can adjust to take account of this new burden by subtracting from the new equity value of the company the present value of all the incremental dividends entailed by the exercise of the warrants:

$$V_2 = V_1 + (W \times E_1) - PV(AD)$$

> where '$PV(AD)$' represents the present value of all of the additional dividends payable as a result of the increased number of shares in issue following exercise of the warrants.

---

[5] An "approximate adjustment" primarily because, as mentioned, dilution adjustments in stock prices should be and normally are made in anticipation of exercise of warrants, where the probability of their exercise should be a variable appearing in the adjustment function. Such a refined approach complicates matters beyond what is desirable here, however.

Note that the pre-exercise equity value of the firm (V_1) is equal to the product of the pre-exercise number of shares (call it N) and the share price before adjustment to take account of the corrosive effect of the warrants (call such share price S_1):

$$V_1 = N \times S_1$$

Further, the value of each share *following* exercise of the warrants (S_2) is simply the post-exercise equity value of the company divided by the post-exercise number of shares in issue:[6]

$$S_2 = \frac{V_2}{(N+W)}$$

Replacing V_2 using the identity derived above we have

$$S_2 = \frac{V_1 + (W \times E_1) - PV(AD)}{(N+W)}$$

Now, replacing V_1 using the appropriate identity derived above, we have

$$S_2 = \frac{N \times S_1 + (W \times E_1) - PV(AD)}{(N+W)} \qquad 10(1)$$

We can make the assumption that, since each warrant among a given issue is identical with all other warrants

[6] An assumption made here is that each warrant is exercisable into one share of stock. It might be too cynical to suggest that underwriters often construct warrants issues such that each warrant represents a call on only a fraction of a share in order to confuse investors. Nevertheless, you should be particularly diligent in confirming what exactly it is that your warrant confers the right to buy.

comprising the issue, the circumstances which make it rational to exercise one warrant will make it rational to exercise all the warrants. In other words, if one warrant is exercised then all are exercised; if one is not exercised then none are exercised.

WHEN NOT TO EXERCISE A WARRANT

We can adapt the argument of Chapter 9 in order to define the conditions which must necessarily obtain before it is rational to exercise a warrant. In that chapter, in the section concerning the comparison of American and European options, it was concluded that it will never be rational to exercise an option if the minimum value of that option unexercised exceeds its value exercised (i.e., in the case of a call, if the minimum value of the call exceeds the value of the underlying commodity less the exercise price).

Defining the Minimum Value of a Warrant

It is trivially true that a warrant will never be less valuable than its intrinsic value as computed after making an anti-dilution adjustment as described above. *'Floor value$_1$'* to a warrant, therefore, is its intrinsic value, or $S_2 - E_1$. But a package comprising an unexercised warrant along with the cash needed to exercise it will often have two important advantages over the underlying stock, making the package more valuable than that underlying stock. The first of these advantages is that the cash component of the package can typically be invested to earn more income than the income (the dividends) accruing on the underlying stock.

Suppose a warrant has n periods to expiration. By deferring exercise of the warrant for the n periods and depositing the exercise price to earn interest the warrant-holder is able to capture this income pick-up. The present value of the pick-up will be reflected in the '*floor value*$_2$' of the warrant:

> *floor value*$_2$ = *intrinsic value of warrant + PV(interest accruing on n period deposit) – PV(n periods of "underlying dividends")*

The intrinsic value of the warrant is $S_2 - E_1$. *PV(interest accruing on n period deposit)*, meanwhile, is simply the present value of (approximately)[7] $[E_1(1+r)^n - E_1]$. Using a discount rate of r, this works out to be $E_1[1-1/(1+r)^n]$. Finally, let us term the n periods of dividends accruing on the underlying stock '$PV(DIVS_{1,..,n})$'. Then we have the *floor value*$_2$ to a warrant expressible as follows:

$$\textit{floor value}_2 = S_2 - E_1 + E_1\left(1 - \frac{1}{(1+r)^n}\right) - PV(DIVS_{1,..,n})$$

We stated above that it will never be rational to exercise a warrant if the minimum value of that warrant *unexercised* exceeds its value exercised (i.e., its intrinsic value). It will thus never be rational to exercise a warrant if, for example, that warrant's *floor value*$_2$ exceeds its intrinsic value. That is, if

$$S_2 - E_1 + E_1\left(1 - \frac{1}{(1+r)^n}\right) - PV\,(DIVS_{1,..,n}) > S_2 - E_1$$

In other words, if

---

7 "Approximately" because in order to match the risk associated with the dividend a portion of E—that portion which represents the excess of E over the present value of E, computed at the riskless discount rate—might be deposited at a rate of R_e—the rate reflecting the risk associated with the dividends. *PV (interest accruing on n period deposit)* in this case would, in fact, amount to $E(1+R_e)^n[1-1/(1+r)^n]/(1+r)^n$.

$$E_1\left(1-\frac{1}{(1+r)^n}\right) > PV(DIVS_{1,..,n})$$

This condition will, of course, *always* obtain where the underlying stock is non-dividend paying, implying that it will never be rational to exercise a warrant into such stock prior to the warrant's expiration.

THE DO-IT-YOURSELF VALUATION OF WARRANTS

Suppose that the condition adduced above obtains and that it is thus rational to defer exercise of the warrants. Now we can value dilutive warrants representing a call on stock using an adaptation of the Do-It-Yourself model, where the adaptation takes into account an anti-dilution adjustment to the value of the underlying stock. If 'C_W' denotes a call warrant's value:

$$C_W = \frac{1}{(1+r)^n}\sum_{j=1}^{T} P_j \times max[(S_j - E_1),0]$$

where

> T is the exhaustive number of possible spot prices of the underlying stock which might prevail at expiration of the warrant;
>
> S_j is the jth such possible spot price of the underlying stock, adjusted to reflect the corrosive effect of the exercise of the warrants. The adjustment is given by Equation 10(1):

$$S_j = \frac{N \times S_u + (W \times E_1) - PV(AD)}{(N+W)}$$

where

N, *W* and *PV(AD)* have the meanings ascribed above, E_1 has the meaning ascribed above (this is repeated for the sake of clarity below), and S_u is the *unadjusted* *j*th possible spot price of the underlying stock, determined just as though the warrants had never been issued;

P_j is the probability that the spot price of the underlying stock prevailing at expiration of the warrant will be S_j (or that the unadjusted price would be S_u);

E_1 is the exercise price of the warrant, and thus $max[(S_j - E_1), 0]$ (i.e., the higher of $S_j - E_1$ and 0) is the warrant's payoff in the event of a price outcome of S_j;

r is the annually compounded riskless interest or discounting rate, expressed in % per compounding period (i.e., % p.a.); and

n is the number of years (i.e., the number of compounding periods) up to the expiration of the warrant.

Note that in applying this model, go for S_u—that is, predict the possible share price outcomes and ascribe them probabilities exactly as though the company concerned had never issued warrants. Then work back from S_u to S_j using the adjustment equation given above under the explanation of 'S_j'.

FINANCING WITH WARRANTS: THE CASE OF THE 'HARMLESS' WARRANTS

Warrants most commonly represent calls on common shares. From time to time corporations and banks have issued warrants which represent calls or puts on currencies, stock market indexes, and other commodities, such as gold and oil. Issues of these instruments typically represent attempts by issuers to take advantage of what they no doubt feel to be a tendency on the part of investors to over-value the warrants. (This is, of course, what capitalists hold to be the normal incentive to sell in a free market system.)

But sometimes the issuance of warrants has simply been intended to assume some exposure which offsets another that exists in the normal course of business. Take, for example, the case of so-called "harmless" warrants issues, several of which were undertaken—principally in the international, or "Eurobond", market—around the mid-1980s.

Now it is not unusual in most capital markets for bonds to be issued with *call features* attaching to them. These call features typically provide for the issuer of the bond to be able, at his option, to buy back or "call" the bonds at a particular redemption or *call price*, sometime before the bonds' specified maturity date. Of course, this feature—as its name suggests—represents no more than a call option residing with the issuer. The bond purchaser has effectively 'sold' the call, for he is the one who must deliver the bond when the call is exercised. The sale of a bond with an issuer's call feature attaching to it could, in other words, be replicated by (i) the sale of a bond without such a feature, along with (ii) the simultaneous sale by the investor to the issuer of an option for the issuer to call that bond at an exercise price equal to the call price.

It was exactly this replication analysis which lay behind the issuance of "harmless" warrants. Harmless warrants were bond warrants (that is, warrants to buy bonds) which were issued in a package along with conventional bonds. The conventional bonds had an issuer's call feature attaching to them. The terms of the warrants, meanwhile, exactly matched the terms of that issuer's call feature. The result was that on the one hand the issuer had the ability to buy back the bonds from investors pursuant to the call feature, while on the other hand the warrant-holders had the ability to buy a new, effectively identical, bond.

Consider a hypothetical example: a corporation seeking ten-year financing issues ten-year Eurobonds incorporating a five-year issuer's call feature, exercisable at a price equal to 105% of the bonds' par value. To each of these "original" bonds is attached a warrant with a five-year expiration and an exercise price of $105 for every $100 principal amount of underlying bond. Each warrant confers on the holder the right to purchase a bond with an identical maturity and with a coupon which is identical to (or perhaps marginally lower than) the coupon of an original bond.

Suppose the warrants represent a European-type option and are thus exercisable only at the end of their five-year life. The sense in which the warrants are "harmless" should be clear: at the end of five years, to the extent the warrants are exercised, the issuer is able to call a corresponding number of original bonds. Since the conditions for exercise of the warrants are that interest rates should be low enough that the underlying bonds are worth more than 105% of their par value, the issuer, by calling the original bonds, thereby avoids a net increase in what would be high cost debt.

The arbitrage embodied in the "harmless" warrants structure is obvious and crude—but not so obvious and crude that several successful financings could not be undertaken. The structure enabled issuers to achieve a lower cost of, in our example, ten-year finance than would have been possible through an issue of ten-year, no-call bonds. It did this because the market undervalued the issuer's call option embedded in the original bonds, relative to the effectively identical call option represented by the warrants.

It might be claimed that an arbitrage involving the purchase of one option and the simultaneous sale of an effectively identical option—but at a higher price—*back to the same person* takes advantage of investor innocence rather than a genuine investment demand. Further, it might be claimed that it adds little or no value to the financial system as a whole. How persuasive this claim would be depends upon whether there exists reason to believe there is value to being able to detach a call option from a host bond.

Chapter 11

11

Convertible Debentures

INTRODUCTION

Typically, convertible debentures (where "convertible debentures" and "convertible bonds" are synonymous terms) are hybrid bond/stock option securities. They have a specified maturity and coupons which represent entitlement to interest, much like a conventional bond. But they also confer on the investor the right to tender the debenture in exchange for a predetermined number of common shares.

While the term "convertible debenture" typically attaches to a debenture that is convertible into the common stock of the issuing company, there are many variations on the theme. Debentures have been issued by one company that are convertible into the stock of another. Debentures have also been issued which are "convertible" into a specified amount of a commodity, such as gold. The "conversion" in this case might either entail (depending on the terms of the issue) tendering the debenture in exchange for delivery of the physical commodity or, more commonly, tendering the debenture for delivery of the then prevailing cash value of the underlying commodity.[1] For the purposes of this chapter we will confine ourselves to conventional common stock convertible debentures. It should be clear, however, that much of what is said is pertinent in relation to (or at least readily adaptable to) most variations on the convertible theme.

The following terms are basic to the analysis of convertible securities:

- the *conversion period* is the period during which, or up to the dates on which, a convertible debenture holder has the right to exercise his conversion privilege;

- the *conversion price* is the par value of a convertible debenture divided by the number of shares into which that debenture may be converted (the number of shares into which a debenture is convertible is sometimes known as the *conversion ratio* of the debenture);

- the *conversion value* of a convertible debenture is the current market value of all of the shares into which that debenture may be converted; and

- the *conversion premium* associated with a convertible debenture is the premium, expressed in per-

[1] Where only cash is deliverable, and not the underlying commodity itself, the debenture is often said to be "indexed" to the underlying commodity, rather than "convertible" into it.

centage points, of the par value or principal amount of that debenture over its conversion value.

THE 'EXERCISE PRICE' OF THE CONVERSION OPTION

The right to convert a debenture—to tender it in exchange for stock—represents a type of call option on the underlying stock. But it is in important respects dissimilar to the calls we have so far considered. Most importantly, the exercise price of this embedded call must be carefully distinguished from the conversion price of the debenture: for the exercise price of an option is really the cash value of what an option holder must give up in order to get possession, through exercise of the option, of the underlying commodity. And what the holder of a convertible debenture gives up when he exercises the conversion privilege is *the debenture itself.* The cash value of the debenture is the present value of all the future cash flows associated with it, computed on the basis of the appropriate 'risky' discount rate. To the extent that the value of the debenture *qua* bond will change as a function of, *inter alia*, discount rates and the remaining life of the debenture, the "exercise price" of the embedded call will similarly fluctuate. This is the reason that a convertible debenture *cannot* be analyzed as two conjoined but essentially distinct instruments—a bond plus an option.[2]

---

[2] Convertible debentures are, in fact, very complex animals, virtually impossible to replicate with packages of 'basic' components. A wholly satisfactory arbitrage pricing analysis is thus hard to achieve. For the purposes of this chapter we will take something a little less than a wholly satisfactory approach by conceiving of convertible debentures as a sort of call on stock *with a fluctuating exercise price*. This is less than wholly satisfactory because options do not, as a matter of definition, have exercise prices which fluctuate with the price of some other commodity—any "option" which does have such a fluctuating exercise price can always be reduced to two or more 'basic' options. A simple characterization of a

As a brief aside, consider the implications of this claim for those issues (which were mentioned in passing in the previous chapter) of warrants, where the exercise price of the warrant can be satisfied by surrender of the bond to which the warrant originally comes attached. If the bond *must* be surrendered in order to effect the exercise (i.e., if the investor does not have the option of using cash to satisfy the exercise price), then the bond with warrant package is exactly analogous to a convertible bond—the warrants are useless without the bond and the bond is not exchangeable for stock without the warrants. If, on the other hand, the exercise price may be satisfied using *either* the bond *or* cash, the bond with warrant package confers an additional option on the holder and is likely to be more valuable than a similarly-couponed debenture which is convertible into the same stock at the same "conversion" price.

WHEN TO EXERCISE THE CONVERSION OPTION?

One of the most troubling questions confronting the convertible debenture investor is when, absent a tender offer for the underlying stock or some other extraordinary circumstance,

---

convertible debenture in terms of more basic options would start as follows. First, there is clearly an investor's stock call option component. Second, and equally clearly, there is a bond-like component. Third, there is an investor's bond put option—an option to put the bond-like component to the issuer in satisfaction of the call option's exercise price. But there is a fourth component, for under certain circumstances—call them conditions *Q*—it may (at this point we have no reason to rule it out) be advantageous for the investor to exercise the conversion privilege even though the bond-like component of the debenture has a fair value which exceeds the exercise price of the call option component. The fourth element in the conceptual replicating package, therefore, is a kind of issuer's option to call the bond-like component when conditions *Q* prevail. Any complete attempt to value convertible debentures must take into account these four components in terms of which such debentures can be characterized, along with other features such as the issuer's call options (options to call the debentures for redemption under certain circumstances) which are common to such securities. Such depth of analysis is, however, well beyond the scope of this chapter.

does it make sense to exercise the conversion option? Again (paralleling the analyses of Chapters 9 and 10) an obvious first point is that it will never be rational to convert a debenture if the minimum value of that debenture *unconverted* exceeds its conversion value.

A debenture's conversion value is, by the definition set forth above, the product of the number of shares into which the debenture is convertible and the prevailing market value of each such share. As in the case of warrants, however, we must make an *anti-dilution adjustment* to the market value of each share to take account of the corrosive effect of the dilution entailed by the conversion.

Making the Anti-Dilution Adjustment

Let us assume, as we did in the analysis of warrants, that if it is rational to convert one debenture then it will be rational to convert every similar debenture. The post-conversion share price, after the dilution adjustment, will be equal to the pre-conversion equity value of the firm, plus the exercise price received from the conversion, less the present value of all the additional dividends payable by the firm as a result of conversion, all divided by the number of shares in issue following conversion.

If B is the principal amount of the debentures and C_p is the conversion price per share associated with them, then B/C_p shares become issuable upon conversion. If N is the number of shares outstanding before conversion, then $N + B/C_p$ are outstanding after conversion. Let us denote the pre-conversion price of each of the underlying shares by 'S_1', the aggregate exercise price of *all* of the debentures by 'E' and the present value of all the dividends associated with the B/C_p shares issuable upon conversion by '$PV(AD)$'. Then S_2, the share price after adjustment to reflect the corrosive effect of conversion of debentures, is given by an equation analogous to Equation 10(1):

$$S_2 = \frac{N \times S_1 + E - PV(AD)}{N + (B/C_p)} \qquad 11(1)$$

The Conversion Value of the Debentures

The conversion value of the debentures is, by our definition, $S_2{\times}B/C_p$.

Computing the "Exercise Price" of the Conversion Option

Now let us focus on the term 'E' in Equation 11(1). It denotes the exercise price of the debentures which, by the definition above, is the present value (computed on the basis of the appropriate 'risky' discount rate) of all of the future cash flows associated with the debentures. Let us split these cash flows into two components. First, on each interest payment date up to, but not including, the maturity of the debentures there will be a coupon payment. If the debentures' coupon is I% per coupon-payment period then each coupon payment will be in the amount of $B \times I$. At maturity of the debentures two amounts are payable. There is the final coupon payment (in an amount of $B \times I$) plus the repayment of principal, in the amount of B. The total payment at maturity is thus $B(1{+}I)$. If the number of interest periods to maturity of the debentures is n we can present value these two cash flow components as follows:

$$PV(coupons\ due\ prior\ to\ maturity) =$$

$$\sum_{j=1}^{n-1} \frac{B \times I}{(1 + R_d)^j}$$

where 'R_d' represents the appropriate discount rate for the discounting of bond cash flows, expressed in percent per discount (coupon payment) period, and

PV(final coupon plus principal repayment) =

$$\frac{B\,(1 + I)}{(1 + R_d)^n}$$

E is simply the sum of these present values:

$$E = \sum_{j=1}^{n-1} \frac{B \times I}{(1 + R_d)^j} + \frac{B(1 + I)}{(1 + R_d)^n} \qquad 11(2)$$

The Minimum Value of a Convertible Debenture

In an exercise analogous to that undertaken in Chapter 9 to determine the minimum value of an option, here we examine the often made claim that the minimum value of a convertible debenture is defined by the higher of just two things, (i) the "exercise price" associated with it—that is, its value *as a bond*—and (ii) its conversion value—that is, its value *as stock.*

The analysis is straightforward. A debenture can be held unconverted and the conversion option simply ignored. Since the conversion option must have a value equal to or greater than zero, that value is obviously greater than (i) above. Further, a convertible debenture can normally be converted into stock at any time[3] (i.e., it typically embodies an American call) and with no cash outlay. Therefore its value will always be greater than (ii) above. That is, a debenture will never be less valuable than the underlying stock (less, perhaps, the cost of transportation to the place the conversion takes place). But debentures typically have advantages over the underlying stock making them—at a minimum—more valuable still. Most importantly, the coupon income to be had from a debenture is normally greater than the dividend income associated with the underlying stock.[4] By deferring exercise of the conversion option for the *n* periods to maturity of the debenture, the investor is able to capture this income pick-up, the present value of which will be reflected in yet a third 'floor' to the value of the debenture:

$$\textit{floor value}_3 = \textit{conversion value} + PV(\textit{coupon income}) - PV(n \textit{ periods of "underlying dividends"}) \qquad 11(3)$$

The conversion value we calculated above was $S_2 \times B/C_p$. *PV(coupon income)*, meanwhile, is simply the present value of all the coupon payments made prior to the maturity of the debentures (the coupon payment due *at* maturity will be lost as the investor converts). This we computed above:

$$PV(\textit{coupons due prior to maturity}) =$$

[3] Note, however, that even if there is the contractual freedom to convert at any time, there is an incentive to do so only on or shortly after coupon dates, or just prior to ex-dividend dates, in order to capture the relevant coupon payment or dividend.

[4] As a further advantage, a debenture confers rights in liquidation which are senior to common stock. Because of the often capricious character of U.S. bankruptcy proceedings, however, such seniority is difficult to value and will be ignored here. One thing debentures do not confer, which shares of stock typically do, is voting rights. Unfortunately, however, such rights are generally of negligible economic value to the portfolio investor and will also be ignored in our analysis.

$$\sum_{j=1}^{n-1} \frac{B \times I}{(1+R_d)^j}$$

Finally, let us term the present value of the n periods of dividends accruing on the underlying stock '$PV(DIVS_{1,..,n})$'. Then, calling the third floor value to a convertible debenture 'DV_{min}', we have

$$DV_{min} = S_2 \frac{B}{C_p} + \sum_{j=1}^{n-1} \frac{B \times I}{(1+R_d)^j} - PV(DIVS_{1,..,n})$$

We started this section by making the point that it will never be rational to convert a debenture if the minimum value of that debenture *unconverted* exceeds its conversion value. In other words, it is a necessary condition of exercise of the conversion option that the conversion value of the debenture is equal to or greater than the minimum value of the debenture unconverted. We have adduced three floors to the value of an unconverted debenture and are thus able to express this necessary condition in three parts:

it will never be rational to convert a debenture unless each of the following three conditions are met:

(i)

$$S_2 \frac{B}{C_p} \geq \sum_{j=1}^{n-1} \frac{B \times I}{(1+R_d)^j} + \frac{B(1+I)}{(1+R_d)^n}$$

(note that B can be divided into each side of the inequality to simplify); *and*

(ii)

$$S_2 \frac{B}{C_p} \geq S_2 \frac{B}{C_p}$$

(this is trivial); *and*

(iii)

$$S_2 \frac{B}{C_p} \geq S_2 \frac{B}{C_p} + \sum_{j=1}^{n-1} \frac{B \times I}{(1+R_d)^j} - PV(DIVS_{1,..,n})$$

Condition (iii) simplifies to

$$PV(DIVS_{1,..,n}) \geq \sum_{j=1}^{n-1} \frac{B \times I}{(1+R_d)^j}$$

Note that condition (iii) *cannot* obtain in the event the underlying stock is non-dividend paying.

THE DO-IT-YOURSELF VALUATION OF CONVERTIBLE DEBENTURES

We can value convertible debentures using an adaptation of the Do-It-Yourself model. Suppose for a moment that at a particular point in time conditions (i) to (iii) above do not all obtain. It will be rational to defer conversion of the debentures, and their valuation should thus be undertaken on the basis of their payoff at maturity. Convertible debentures differ from options (including warrants) in that no cash outlay is entailed in the event they are converted. At maturity the debenture-holder receives the higher of (a) the debenture's then prevailing conversion value (without deduction of any cash outlay) or (b) the sum of the debenture's principal value and the final coupon payment due. In other words:

$$Maturity\ payoff = max[(S_n \times B/C_p), B(1+I)]$$

where S_n is the then prevailing spot price of one share of the underlying stock, adjusted to reflect the corrosive effect on the stock price of dilution.

We can now simply plug this payoff expression into the Do-It-Yourself model in order to adapt the model to the valuation of convertible debentures. If 'C_b' denotes the fair value of the entire issue of convertible debentures, then

$$C_b = \frac{1}{(1+r)^n} \sum_{j=1}^{T} P_j \times max[(S_j \times B/C_p), B(1+I)] \qquad 11(4)$$

where

T is the exhaustive number of possible spot prices of the underlying stock which might prevail at maturity of the debenture;

S_j is the jth such possible spot price of one share of the underlying stock, adjusted to reflect the corrosive effect on the stock price of dilution. The anti-dilution adjustment is given by Equation 11(1):

$$S_j = \frac{N \times S_u + E - PV(AD)}{N + (B/C_p)}$$

where

N, E, $PV(AD)$, B and C_p have the meanings ascribed above and S_u is the *unadjusted* jth possible spot price of one share of the underlying stock, determined just as though the convertible debentures had never been issued;

P_j is the probability that the spot price of the underlying stock prevailing at maturity of the debenture will be S_j (or that the unadjusted price would be S_u);

B is the aggregate number of shares into which the debentures are convertible;

I is the amount of each coupon payment due in respect of the debentures, expressed as a percentage of the debentures' par value, and hence $B(1+I)$ is the total interest and principal payment due at maturity of the debentures. $max[(S_j \times B/C_p), B(1+I)]$ is thus the debenture's payoff in the event of a price outcome of S_j;

r is the annually compounded riskless interest or discounting rate, expressed in % per compounding or interest period; and,

n is the number of compounding or interest periods up to the maturity of the debenture.

CONVERTIBLE DEBENTURES IN THE REAL WORLD

Footnoted earlier in this chapter is the claim that convertible debentures are very complex animals. In the real world they are often issued with features that complicate the analysis we have so far undertaken. The remainder of this chapter is devoted to a description of these complicating features and to an analysis of the way in which convertible debentures are typically used by companies as financing vehicles.

The Impact of an Issuer's Call

One omission from the analysis so far is consideration of an important feature, common to most convertible bonds—viz, an issuer's call option, providing for the issuer's ability to call the bonds for redemption prior to their specified maturity. Such a call feature is often used to force investors to convert into stock before they would otherwise be inclined to do so. And a call is an efficient way of inducing conversion when the conversion value of the bonds exceeds the call price—for by converting during the notice period the issuer is required to give in connection with the call, the investor at least gets the underlying stock, rather than having to settle for the (lower) call price.

Typically there will be constraints placed upon an issuer with respect to his ability to exercise his call option. Most commonly, the call option will be exercisable within, say, five years of the issue of the debentures *only if the conversion value of the debentures exceeds a specified 'hurdle' price* (say, 140% of the debentures' principal amount). This constraint keeps an issuing company from selling debentures, waiting until the conversion value of those debentures approaches the call price, and then calling them for redemption. Such a scheme would result in the issuer simply enjoying the benefits of low-cost debt for a period at the expense of debenture-holders.

An issuer's call is simply a call option on convertible debentures. The value of the underlying commodity—the debentures themselves—is given by Equation 11(4). The value of convertible debentures embodying an issuer's call is thus

$C_b - C_{Cb}$, where C_{Cb} is the fair value of the issuer's call option as we have described it above—that is, a call on an underlying commodity, the value of which is given by C_b. The claim that convertible debentures are very complex animals is borne out as soon as the analyst embarks on an attempt to compute $C_b - C_{Cb}$.

Why Do Companies Issue Convertible Debentures?

It is sometimes maintained that the issuance of convertible debentures represents a win-win proposition for the issuing company: if the debentures are eventually converted, the company will have effectively sold stock at an above-market price (remember that the conversion price is set at a premium to the market price of the underlying stock at issuance). On the other hand, if the debentures expire unconverted the issuing company will simply have benefited from low-cost debt (remember that the coupon on convertible debentures is set at below the issuing company's normal borrowing rate to reflect the benefit to investors of the conversion option).

If there was any merit at all to this claim, convertible debenture issues would, of course, be far more common than they are (or, at least, there would be far more evidence of companies trying to issue such instruments). The truth, for the issuer, is that convertible debentures might as well be characterized as high-dividend paying stock as they might as high priced stock (the "high dividends" in part account for the "high price"). Further, if the debentures remain unconverted it is likely to be far from good news to the issuer—it is likely that this reflects a poor performance on the part of the issuing company—the very circumstances under which a debt repayment burden is least welcome.

The Value to Investors of 'Downside Protection'

We concluded in Chapter 9 that the real value to the buyer of conventional call options lies (counter-intuitively) in the *downside protection* they confer. It is tempting to say the same about convertible debentures: as we saw above, convertible debentures will never be less valuable than the present value of the cash flows they confer, and neither will they ever be less valuable than their conversion value. Moreover, we saw that their minimum value will exceed their conversion value so long as the present value of their coupon stream exceeds the present value of the dividends payable on the underlying stock over the same period (see Equation 11(3)). But now examine this last floor to a convertible debenture's value. It is given by the equation derived above:

$$DV_{min} = \frac{S_2 \times B}{C_p} + \sum_{j=1}^{n-1} \frac{B \times I}{(1+R_d)^j} - PV(DIVS_{1,..,n})$$

Suppose the issuing company performs badly. "Never mind," says the debenture-holder, "I'm still better off than I would have been had I bought either the stock itself or the issuer's conventional bonds." Alas, not necessarily so. First, consider the debenture-holder's position relative to that of a holder of stock: the worse the issuing company performs, the higher the discount rate appropriate to the valuation of its debt—in other words, the higher R_d in the equation. As R_d tends to infinity (∞) so the 'Σ' expression in the equation tends to 0, and DV_{min} tends to $S_2 \times B/C_p - PV(DIVS_{1,..,n})$. But a poorly performing company seldom pays dividends, hence the worse the company performs the closer DV_{min} approaches to the conversion value of $S_2 \times B/C_p$. Someone who had, at the time of issuance of the debentures for B, spent an amount of

B on the underlying stock rather than on the debentures would, meanwhile, have purchased B/S_1 shares. His position now has a market value of $S_2 \times B/S_1$.

Now it is clear that the value of the stockholder's position may in some cases exceed DV_{min}. That is, it may be the case that $S_2 \times B/S_1 > DV_{min}$, for this implies that

$$S_2 \frac{B}{S_1} > S_2 \frac{B}{C_p}$$

or, expressed another way, that

$$C_p > S_1$$

where 'C_p' denotes the conversion price per share associated with the debentures and 'S_1' denotes the price per share of the underlying stock at issuance of the debentures. And, of course, *C_p will always be greater than S_1*, since this is what is entailed by issuing convertible debentures at a conversion *premium.*

Now, let us turn our attention to a consideration of the debenture-holder's position relative to that of a holder of conventional bonds. In this case it is equally clear that the debenture-holder may be the worse off, for at worst neither the debentures nor the issuing company's conventional bonds have any residual value at all. In this case, the holder of the conventional bonds would, at least, have enjoyed higher interest, while it had been paid, than the debenture-holder.

Chapter 12

12

Constructing an Option Pricing Model

THE ONE-PERIOD BINOMIAL OPTION PRICING FORMULA

XYZ Inc. common shares pay no dividends. They currently trade at S per share. The XYZ share price has always followed a very regular pattern of growth. During the coming year, however, you—as an XYZ shareholder—anticipate a watershed in the company's development, as a major new product line will be brought to the market. The probability (p) that the new product line will prove successful you estimate at 60%. If it is successful, the XYZ share price will continue to grow and will, you are convinced, move upward by a factor of u during the coming year.

There is, or course, a 40% (i.e., a $1-p$) probability that XYZ's new product line will prove unsuccessful. If it is unsuccessful, then you confidently predict a drop in the company's share price during the coming year by a factor of d. The possible XYZ share price outcomes after the coming year are as seen in Figure 12–1.

A European call option into XYZ common shares is available with one year to expiration. The value of the call one year hence will be the higher of either its intrinsic value or zero. Thus, if the new XYZ product line is successful and the XYZ share price moves up, the value of the call (C_u), one year hence, will be the higher of $u.S - E$ and zero:

$$C_u = max(u.S - E, 0)$$

If the new product line fails and the XYZ share price drops, the value of the call (C_d) one year hence will be the higher of $d.S - E$ and zero:

Figure 12—1

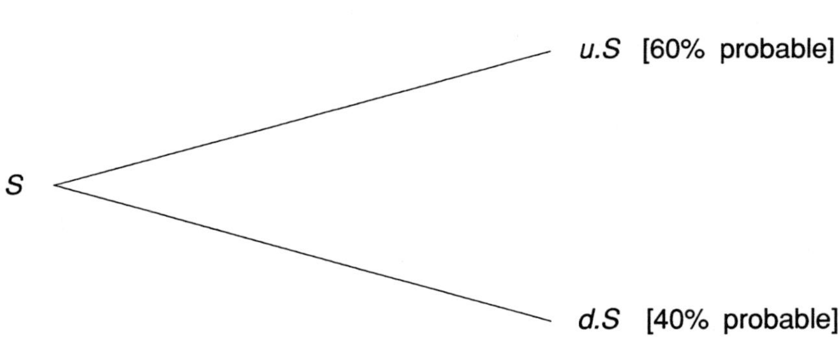

$$C_d = max(d.S - E, 0)$$

C_u represents the payoff of the call in the 60% probable event that XYZ shares rise in price to *u.S*, while C_d represents the payoff of the call in the 40% probable event that XYZ shares drop in price to *d.S*. In Chapter 7, we showed that the value of an entitlement to a contingent payoff is equal to the product of the amount of that payoff and the probability that it will be received. This relationship we termed, "the basic price-payoff relationship." In the XYZ case, we have shown that the payoff of the call will be either C_u or C_d. The call, in effect, represents two component bets, one on a *u.S* price outcome, in which case the payoff is C_u, and another on a *d.S* price outcome, in which case the payoff is C_d. The value of the call must thus be the aggregate of the value of these two component bets.

The value of an entitlement to a payoff of C_u, which is p probable, is $C_u p$. The value of an entitlement to a payoff of C_d, which is $(1-p)$ probable, is $C_d(1-p)$. The value of the contingent entitlement to one or other of these mutually exclusive and exhaustive payoffs is thus $C_u p + C_d(1-p)$. This is the amount an investor should be willing to pay for the contingent entitlement to an immediate payoff of either C_u or C_d. As represented by the call, however, the payoff will not be received until one year from now when the option expires. Hence, the aggregate value of the contingent bets which comprise the call have to be present-valued in order to derive what the investor should be willing to pay for the call today. This PV should, assuming no credit risk is associated with the call, be calculated on the basis of the riskless interest rate. Thus,

$$C = \frac{C_u p + C_d(1-p)}{(1+r)^1} \qquad 12(1)$$

where

C is the value of the call one period prior to its expiration; and

r is the riskless annually compounded interest rate, expressed in % per year.

This is the one-period European call option pricing formula for non-income bearing commodities.

ARBITRAGE PRICING OF CALL OPTIONS

We can adopt a different methodology and use an arbitrage pricing approach similar to that used in the analysis of futures pricing, in order to arrive at Equation 12(1).

Consider once more the stock of ABC, which is currently trading at \$100 per share (i.e., S = \$100) and which pays a dividend annually of \$5 per share. Like XYZ, ABC has just introduced a new product, which may or may not succeed. If the new product is a success, you—as an investment analyst—are 100% convinced that the stock, one year hence, will be trading at \$110 per share. You are also 100% convinced, however, that should the product fail, the stock will be trading at \$90. If there are one-year European calls into ABC common stock trading in the marketplace, how will you be able to take advantage of your assessment of future price outcomes to exploit any profit opportunity?

The calls' exercise price is \$100 per share and each call, exercisable into one share of stock, is trading at a price of C. If you buy two calls, your possible cash flows will be as set forth in Figure 12–2.

Suppose the one-year riskless interest rate is 6% p.a. and the one-year rate reflecting the same amount of risk as that attaching to the ABC dividend is 7% p.a. Using the expanded general forward and futures pricing equation (Equation 4(1)), we can determine that a one-year forward position in one ABC share will have no value (i.e., $c = 0$) when the forward price (f) associated with the contract is \$101.05:

$$f = (1.06)^1 \left(\$100 - \frac{\$5}{(1.07)^1} \right)$$

Now consider what would happen if, simultaneously to the purchase of the two ABC calls, you were to sell, for its fair value of zero, a one-year ABC forward contract with a forward price of \$101.05. Your possible cash flows under the forward contract will be as shown in Figure 12–3.

Note that if the ABC stock price is \$110 one year hence, your payoff of minus \$8.95 is \$20 lower than the payoff in the event of a \$90 stock price outcome. Note, also, that this \$20 difference would exactly offset the \$20 payoff that would be associated with the purchase of two calls. In other words,

Figure 12–2

	Cash Flows	
Year	**Future Stock Price = \$110**	**Future Stock Price = \$90**
0	<2C>	<2C>
1	Options exercised; payoff: \$220 – \$200 = \$20	0 (Options unexercised)

Figure 12–3

	Cash Flows	
Year	**Future Stock Price = $110**	**Future Stock Price = $90**
0	0	0
1	Buy share: <$110>	Buy share: <$90>
	Forward price: $101.05	Forward price: $101.05
	Net: <$8.95>	Net: $11.05

if you were to sell the one forward contract (take a short forward position) and simultaneously purchase two of the calls, your cash flows will be identical, whether ABC's new product succeeds or not (see Figure 12–4).

The payoff of a portfolio comprising the two calls and the one share sold forward is $11.05, whatever the ABC stock price outcome. This payoff replicates a one-year deposit which matures in an amount of $11.05. The cost of the portfolio—*2C*—must therefore equal the cost of such a replicating portfolio comprising the deposit. In other words, *2C* must be equal to the present value of $11.05. If no risk attaches to the forward position, then the appropriate discount rate for computing this PV will be the riskless rate of 6% p.a. Hence,

$$2C = PV(\$11.05)$$

Figure 12–4

	Cash Flows					
	Future Stock Price = $110			Future Stock Price = $90		
Year	Options	Forward	Net	Options	Forward	Net
0	<2C>	0	<2C>	<2C>	0	<2C>
1	$20	<$8.95>	$11.05	0	$11.05	$11.05

$$= \$11.05/(1.06)^1$$

Therefore,

$$C = \$5.21$$

Five dollars and twenty-one cents is the unique no-arbitrage price of the one-year call on one ABC common share, exercisable at $100. How should a mispricing be exploited to create an arbitrage profit? The answer to this sort of question is always the same: by selling the overpriced portfolio and buying the cheaper replicating portfolio. If the calls sell for more than $5.21, then you should (i) sell two calls, (ii) buy a one-year forward contract with a forward price of $101.05, and (iii) deposit the PV of $11.05 in a one-year riskless investment earning 6% p.a. Your up-front profit will be the amount by which the two calls are overpriced. One year hence, your net cash flow will be zero, whether the ABC share price at that time is $110 or $90.

THE HEDGE RATIO

In the above arbitrage pricing example, the ratio of calls to forward contracts in the deposit-replicating portfolio is 2:1. The payoff of a portfolio comprising a different ratio of calls to forward contracts would fail to replicate a deposit. Knowing the possible price outcomes associated with ABC shares, how do we determine the ratio—call it H—of calls purchased to shares sold forward that will be required to create a deposit-replicating portfolio?

We want to achieve a portfolio of calls and short forward contracts which will afford the same payoff whether the price of ABC shares moves by a factor of u or by a factor of d over the year. Consider, first, the forward contracts. Under each forward contract, you are obligated to deliver one share for a forward price of f. This share will be purchased by you on the delivery date at its then prevailing price. In the event the prevailing price is $u.S$, the payoff associated with each short forward contract will be $(f - u.S)$. If, however, the prevailing price of the ABC share is $d.S$, then the payoff associated with each short forward contract will be $(f - d.S)$.

Now consider the calls. For each share sold forward the deposit-replicating portfolio will contain H calls. In the event the prevailing ABC share price one year hence is $u.S$, the payoff associated with H calls will be HC_u. If, however, the ABC share price outcome is $d.S$, the payoff associated with the H calls will be HC_d. The deposit-replicating portfolio comprising the short forward contracts plus H calls will thus have an aggregate payoff

(i) in the event the ABC share price one year hence is $u.S$, of $(f - u.S) + HC_u$, and

(ii) in the event the ABC share price one year hence is $d.S$, of $(f - d.S) + HC_d$.

Remember, we wish to determine H such that the payoff of the portfolio will be the same whether the ABC share price outcome is $u.S$ or $d.S$. In other words, we want to find H such that

$$(f - u.S) + HC_u = (f - d.S) + HC_d$$

This is a matter of simple algebra:

$$H = \frac{S(u-d)}{C_u - C_d} \qquad 12(2)$$

H is termed the *hedge ratio* of the deposit-replicating portfolio and is such that the payoff of the portfolio comprising H calls per share sold in the forward market will be the same whether the ABC share price outcome is $u.S$ or $d.S$. The aggregate up-front cost of this portfolio is HC. Since the payoff of the portfolio is not dependent upon the ABC share price outcome (it only depends upon the seller of the calls not defaulting), HC must be equal to the PV of the payoff of the portfolio, discounted at the rate which reflects the risk of default:

$$HC = PV(\,(f - u.S) + HC_u)$$

Since exchange-traded options typically carry negligible risk of default, the appropriate discount rate is the riskless rate of r% p.a.:

$$HC = \frac{(f - u.S) + HC_u}{(1{+}r)^1}$$

Therefore,

$$C = \frac{HC_u + f - u.S}{H(1{+}r)^1}$$

We can substitute for f using the expanded general forward and futures pricing equation (Equation 4(1)). We are dealing with one period (that is, $n = 1$), hence,

$$f = (1{+}r)^1\left(S - \frac{CF_1}{(1{+}R)^1} - C\right)$$

For simplicity, let us substitute A for $(1{+}r)$ and B for $(1{+}R)$ and assume that the forward contract in our deposit replicating portfolio has a forward price, *f*, such that the value of the contract, *c*, is zero. We now have

$$C = \frac{HC_u{+}SA{-}u.S}{HA} - \frac{CF_1}{HB}$$

$$= \frac{HC_u{+}S(A{-}u)}{HA} - \frac{CF_1}{HB}$$

Substituting for *H* from Equation 12(2),

$$C = \frac{S(u{-}d)\ C_u{+}S(A{-}u)\ (C_u{-}C_d)}{AS(u{-}d)} - \frac{CF_1\ (C_u{-}C_d)}{BS(u{-}d)}$$

$$= \frac{1}{A}\left(C_u \frac{(A{-}d)}{(u{-}d)} + C_d \frac{(u{-}A)}{(u{-}d)}\right) - \frac{CF_1\ (C_u{-}C_d)}{BS(u{-}d)}$$

$$= \frac{1}{A}\left(C_u \frac{(A{-}d)}{(u{-}d)} + C_d \left(1 - \frac{(u{-}A)}{(u{-}d)}\right)\right) - \frac{CF_1(C_u{-}C_d)}{BS(u{-}d)} \qquad 12(3)$$

This is the one-period call option pricing equation. Suppose we are dealing with a non-income bearing underlying commodity, such as the XYZ common shares we looked at at the beginning of this chapter. In this case, $CF_1 = 0$, and Equation 12(3) becomes

$$= \frac{1}{A}\left(C_u \frac{(A{-}d)}{(u{-}d)} + C_d \left(1 - \frac{(A{-}d)}{(u{-}d)}\right)\right) \qquad 12(4)$$

Now something very interesting emerges. Recall Equation 12(1), which we derived using the basic price-payoff relationship for pricing calls on non-income bearing commodities. Substituting *A* for (1+*r*) once again, Equation 12(1) becomes

$$C = \frac{1}{A}\left(C_u p + C_d(1-p)\right) \qquad 12(1a)$$

Now equating Equations 12(1a) and 12(4) we have

$$\frac{1}{A}\left(C_u p + C_d(1-p)\right) = \frac{1}{A}\left(C_u \frac{(A-d)}{(u-d)} + C_d\left(1 - \frac{(A-d)}{(u-d)}\right)\right)$$

Notice that both sides of this equality are of the same basic form. Equating the right sides of Equations 12(1a) and 12(4) readily shows that

$$p = \frac{(A-d)}{(u-d)}$$

This result is, in a sense, a cornerstone of modern option-pricing theory. It is often pointed out that modern option-pricing models enable us to eliminate all elements that are somehow subjective from the valuation or pricing process. In the case of our one-period model, the case would go like this:

"Consider the significance of the above equation, expressing p as a function of A, d and u. In deriving Equation 12(1), 'p' represented the probability that the price of the underlying commodity would change by a factor of u during the period. In other words, p embodies 'subjective' expectations or projections concerning the future price of the underlying commodity. The term $(A-d)/(u-d)$ in Equation 12(4), however, embodies no such expectations: in deriving Equation 12(4), we did not have to assess the relative likelihood of a price change by a factor of u rather than by a factor of d. We have, in other words, derived in Equation 12(4) a one-period pricing model that eliminates all references to expectations and, indeed, to all 'subjective' terms whatever."

It is difficult to find anything kind to say about this line of argument. The argument is spurious because Equation 12(4) can only be derived by making certain assumptions about future price outcomes—in our case, for example, we made the assumption that only two possible price outcomes exist at the end of the period. This constraint, of course, does indeed embody some sort of an expectation.

A TWO-PERIOD OPTION PRICING FORMULA

Very rarely—if ever—will we encounter a real-life situation in which the exhaustive possible price outcomes associated with a commodity one year hence are limited to two. But what if we look at possible outcomes not over a period of a year, but over a much shorter period, '*t*'? By assuming that at the end of each such period the price of the commodity in question will have assumed one of only two possible values, we can plot possible price outcomes in a way that can provide for a close approximation to the actual price behavior of a commodity. To see this, suppose we look at discrete periods of one minute. A non-income bearing commodity is currently priced at *S*—say, $100. After one minute, its price will be either 1.1*S* or 0.9*S*. After each subsequent minute, its price will have changed by a factor of either 1.1 ('*u*', as the up-factor was denoted earlier) or 0.9 ('*d*'). Notice that we are dealing with relative, as opposed to absolute, price fluctuations.

After 4 minutes our model provides for the commodity to have assumed any one of five possible prices, ranging from a high of $u^4.S$ (i.e., $146.41) to a low of $d^4.S$ (i.e., $65.61). (See Figure 12–5.)

Any commodity capable of fluctuating to the extremes described by our model—capable, that is, either of gaining 46 percent in value, or of losing 34 percent in value in four discrete price-change periods of one minute each—would, of course, be deemed highly *volatile*.

Figure 12–5

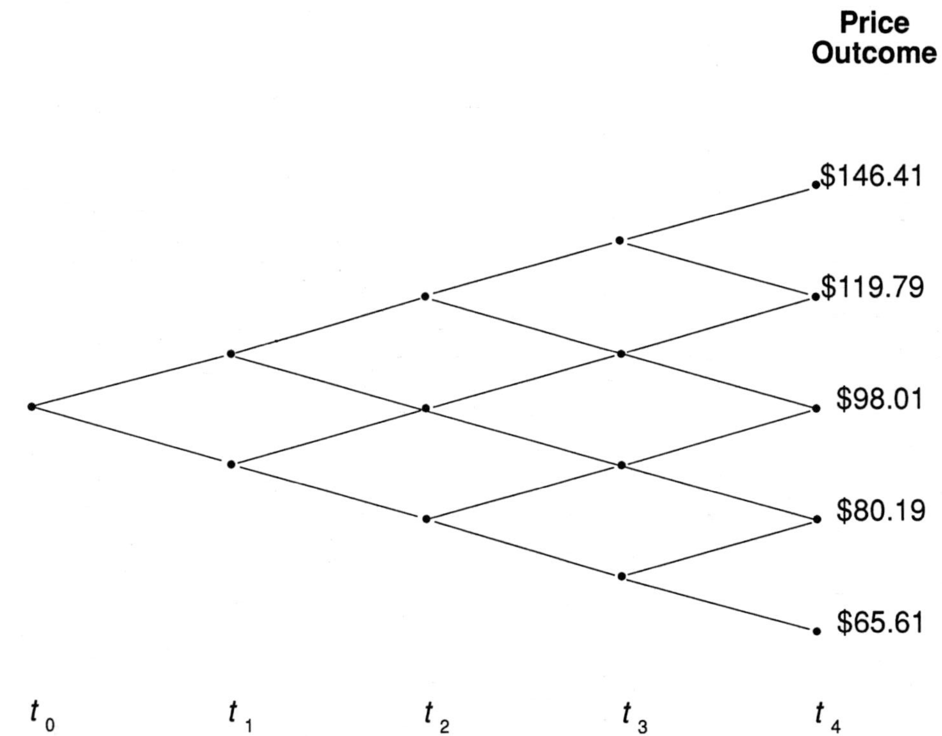

Let us extend the one-period European call option pricing formula and focus on the two periods between t_0 and t_2. One period before expiration of the period we are considering—i.e., at t_1—the price of the underlying commodity will be either $u.S$ or $d.S$. If the price is $u.S$, then the value of the call at that point (call it V_{Cu}), will be given by the one-period option pricing formula (Equation 12(1a)):

$$V_{Cu} = \frac{1}{A}\left(C_{uu}p + C_{ud}(1-p)\right)$$

where

$$C_{uu} = max(u^2.S - E, 0); \text{ and}$$

$$C_{ud} = max(u.d.S - E, 0)$$

Similarly, if the commodity is worth $d.S$ at t_1 then the value of the call at that point (V_{Cd}) is given by

$$V_{Cd} = \frac{1}{A}\left(C_{ud}p + C_{dd}(1-p)\right)$$

where

$$C_{dd} = max(d^2.S - E, 0); \text{ and (as above)}$$

$$C_{ud} = max(u.d.S - E, 0)$$

V_{Cu} and V_{Cd} represent the two possible values of the call at t_1. These values are analogous to the C_u and C_d expressions in Equation 10(1); whereas C_u and C_d represent the value of the call at its expiration (i.e., its then intrinsic value), V_{Cu} and V_{Cd} represent the value of the call one period prior to its expiration. Using Equation 12(1a) once more, we can find the value of the call (V_C) at t_0:

$$V_C = \frac{1}{A}\left(V_{Cu}p + V_{Cd}(1-p)\right)$$

$$= \frac{1}{A^2}\left(p[C_{uu}p + C_{ud}(1-p)] + [1-p][C_{ud}p + C_{dd}(1-p)]\right)$$

$$= \frac{1}{A^2}\left(p^2C_{uu} + 2p(1-p)C_{ud} + (1-p)^2C_{dd}\right) \qquad 12(5)$$

This is the two-period European call option pricing formula for non-income bearing commodities.

THE MULTI-PERIOD BINOMIAL OPTION PRICING MODEL

Equation 12(5) can be modified to deal with expirations in excess of two periods. Consider an option with n periods to expiration. At the end of n periods, the possible price outcomes associated with the underlying commodity, assuming once more that it moves in price by a factor of either u or d during each period, are (starting at the lowest possible outcome) $d^n.S$; $u^1.d^{n-1}.S$; $u^2.d^{n-2}.S$; ....; $u^{n-1}.d^1.S$; $u^n.S$.

These price outcomes can be expressed as $u^a.d^{n-a}.S$, where $a = 0$ and all integral numbers from 1 to n, inclusive. At the end of n periods, the price outcome $u^a.d^{n-a}.S$ will obtain when there have been a periods during which the price of the commodity has changed by a factor of u and $n–a$ periods during which it has changed by a factor of d.

The payoff of a call after n periods—i.e., the option's intrinsic value at expiration—will be the higher of (i) the then current market value of the commodity ($u^a.d^{n-a}.S$) less the exercise price, or (ii) zero. If we call this payoff $C[u^a.d^{n-a}.S]$, then

$$C[u^a.d^{n-a}.S] = max(u^a.d^{n-a}.S - E, 0)$$

$C[u^a.d^{n-a}.S]$ is the payoff of a call after n periods, where the price of the underlying commodity has changed by a factor of u during a periods and by a factor of d during n-a periods.

Knowing n, and hence each possible payoff as a function of u and d, we can invoke the basic price-payoff relationship to determine the value of the contingent entitlement to each such payoff, exactly as we did in deriving the Do-It-Yourself option pricing model in Chapter 8. This value is the product of the payoff in question and the probability of that payoff being received—i.e., the product of the payoff in question and the probability of the price outcome which affords such payoff actually obtaining. But in the case of a call with multiple ($n > 1$) periods to expiration, how do we determine the probability of a particular price outcome?

Again we start by supposing that over any one period there is a probability of p of a price change by a factor of u and thus a probability of (1–p) of a price change by a factor of d. After one period the probability of a $u.S$ price outcome is p and that of a $d.S$ outcome is (1–p). What about after two periods?

It is clear from Figure 12–6 that the probability of a $u^2.S$ outcome is p^2, while that of a $d^2.S$ outcome is $(1–p)^2$. Each of these outcomes would require the factor of change to be the same over each period, u and then u again (probability: p and then p again, or p^2) to arrive at a $u^2.S$ outcome, and d and then d again (probability: (1–p) and then (1–p) again, or $(1–p)^2$) to arrive at a $d^2.S$ outcome. What about the $u.d.S$ outcome? Well, there are two possible paths to this outcome: there is a path which entails a change by a factor of u and then, in the following period, by d (probability: p and then (1–p), or p(1–p)); also, there is a path which entails a change by a factor

Figure 12–6

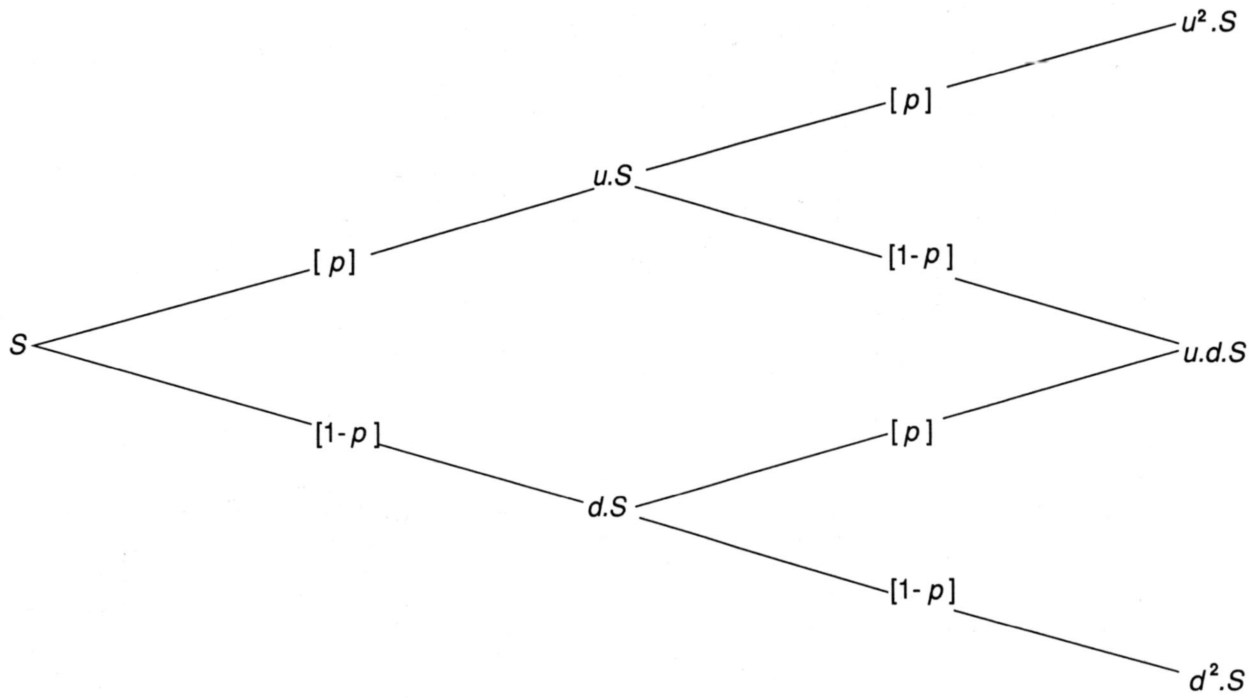

of d and then by u (probability: $(1-p)$ and then p, or $(1-p)p$). The aggregate probability that attaches to this outcome is the sum of these component probabilities, or $2p(1-p)$.

The probability of a price outcome of $u^a.d^{n-a}.S$ is a function of the number of possible paths to that outcome. In particular, it is a function of the number of possible u-steps and d-steps to the outcome. Conveniently, there is a simple formula for computing this probability (which we will call $P_R(u^a.d^{n-a}.S)$). It is known as the Binomial Formula and it tells us that:

$$P_R(u^a.d^{n-a}.S) = \frac{n!}{(n-a)!a!}\, p^a(1-p)^{n-a}$$

where

p is the probability of a price change by a factor of u in any period;

$(1-p)$ is the probability of a price change by a factor of d in any period; and

$y!$ ("y factorial") is the product of all the integers from 1 to y, inclusive (i.e. $1 \times 2 \times 3 .... \times (y-1) \times y$).

Now we have the probability of each possible price outcome (that is, we have found $P_R(u^a.d^{n-a}.S)$ for each possible value of a) we need to multiply it with the payoff that would be received if that price outcome were to obtain (i.e., with the corresponding $C[u^a.d^{n-a}.S]$). Summing these products will give the future value of the option, $FV(C)$, at the point of its expiration:

$$FV(C) = \sum_{a=0}^{n} \left(P_R(u^a.d^{n-a}.S) \times C[u^a.d^{n-a}.S\,] \right)$$

Therefore,

$$C = \frac{1}{A^n} \sum_{a=0}^{n} \left(P_R(u^a.d^{n-a}.S) \times C[u^a.d^{n-a}.S\,] \right)$$

Substituting the Binomial Formula we get:

$$C = \frac{1}{A^n} \sum_{a=0}^{n} \frac{n!}{(n-a)!a!}\, p^a(1-p)^{n-a}.max(u^a.d^{n-a}.S-E,\, 0) \qquad 12(6)$$

This is the multi-period Binomial Option Pricing Model for call options on non-income bearing commodities. The equation is a lot less complicated than it may appear at first sight. In applying it, remember that A is $(1+r)$, where r is the riskless interest rate, expressed in percent per period and compounded once per period.

For our purposes—achieving a critical understanding of the principles of option pricing—the important thing is not to memorize the Binomial Model, but to become familiar with the methodology that leads to it.

At this point, think back to Chapter 8 and how we there applied the basic price-payoff relationship in order to derive the Do-It-Yourself option pricing model. The similarity between the Binomial and Do-It-Yourself models should be striking. In fact, the only difference is that the Binomial Model has built into it a distribution of future possible price outcomes—a *binomial* probability distribution. This imposes limitations. The Do-It-Yourself option pricing model, however, leaves you—the analyst—free to determine the probabilities which attach to various future price outcomes. It places additional responsibility on the user's shoulders, but at the same time it confers more freedom and an ability to factor-in strongly (and hopefully rationally) held beliefs about future events.

Chapter 13

13

The Continuous-Time Option Pricing Model

INTRODUCTION

The Binomial Model for option pricing entails analyzing price movements in the underlying commodity in terms of discrete periods over each of which the price of the underlying commodity is deemed to have changed by one of only two possible factors. By reducing the length of each discrete period to a very short term we can provide for binomial paths that closely describe a wide variety of price movements.

The continuous-time option pricing model provides for a continuum of price changes and possible price outcomes and, in the case of the model for non-income bearing commodities, can be shown to be equivalent to the limiting case of the Binomial Model, as the duration, *t*, of each discrete period approaches zero. It is known as the "Black-Scholes Model," after those who first derived it in the early 1970s.

The derivation of the Black-Scholes Model involves some complicated mathematics. However, we can inch towards it in steps, the logic of which should be comprehensible to most readers. Our starting point (though not that of Black and Scholes when they first derived the model) is the Binomial Model.

Let us start by making some simple re-arrangements of the Binomial Model which appears as Equation 12(6). The '*max(.)*' expression in that equation represents the payoff of the call option in the event of a price outcome of $u^a.d^{n-a}.S$:

$$C[u^a.d^{n-a}.S] = max(u^a.d^{n-a}.S - E, 0)$$

Now there may be some price outcomes—values for $u^a.d^{n-a}.S$—at which $C[u^a.d^{n-a}.S]$ is equal to zero. This will be the case when the price outcome is less than or equal to E (the exercise price of the call). In determining the value of the call, however, we are interested in price outcomes which produce payoffs in excess of zero, since only these, when multiplied by their attendant probabilities, will yield products above zero and thus contribute to the option price. Let us assume that payoffs in excess of zero are only obtained when the price of the underlying commodity has moved by a factor of u more than m times. In other words:

$$u^m.d^{n-m}.S = E$$

and

$$C[u^a.d^{n-a}.S] > 0 \text{ when } a > m$$

We can now modify the Binomial Model, summing only the products of each payoff higher than zero and its corresponding probability:

$$C = \frac{1}{A^n} \sum_{a=m}^{n} \frac{n!}{(n-a)!a!} p^a(1-p)^{n-a} (u^a.d^{n-a}.S-E)$$

The right hand of this equality, in turn, can be re-written as follows:

$$S\left[\sum_{a=m}^{n} \frac{n!}{(n-a)!a!} p^a(1-p)^{n-a} \frac{u^a.d^{n-a}}{A^n}\right]$$
$$-\frac{E}{A^n}\left[\sum_{a=m}^{n} \frac{n!}{(n-a)!a!} p^a(1-p)^{n-a}\right]$$

Now consider the expressions in the square brackets. The second of these expressions is simply the sum of the probabilities—the aggregate probability—of a price outcome which entails *m* or more price moves by a factor of *u* from among a total of *n* price moves. We can re-write this probability function:

$$P_R(m;n,p)$$

meaning, "the probability of *m* successes (i.e., price moves by a factor of *u*) from a total of *n* trials (i.e., from a total of *n* price moves), given a probability of success in any one trial (i.e., a probability of any one price move being by a factor of *u*) of *p*."

The first square-bracketed expression is similar. Let us focus on the latter part of this expression:

$$p^a(1-p)^{n-a}\frac{u^a.d^{n-a}}{A^n}$$

This can be re-written:

$$\left(\frac{u.p}{A}\right)^a\left(\frac{d(1-p)}{A}\right)^{n-a}$$

Recall that in the foregoing chapter, in discussing the hedge ratio in the context of one-period option pricing, we produced two equations—Equations 12(1a) and 12(4)—which, when compared, suggested that

$$p=\frac{(A-d)}{(u-d)}$$

and hence that

$$(1-p)=\frac{(u-A)}{(u-d)}$$

We can plug this result into the above, to produce:

$$\left(\frac{u.p}{A}\right)^a\left(\frac{d(u-A)}{A(u-d)}\right)^{n-a}$$

from which

$$\left(\frac{u.p}{A}\right)^a\left(1-\frac{u(A-d)}{A(u-d)}\right)^{n-a}$$

from which, in turn

$$\left(\frac{u.p}{A}\right)^{a}\left(1-\frac{u.p}{A}\right)^{n-a}$$

Replacing $u.p/A$ with p_1 we have

$$p_1{}^{a}(1-p_1)^{n-a}$$

The first square-bracketed expression from the re-written Binomial Model, thus, becomes

$$\left[\sum_{a=m}^{n}\frac{n!}{(n-a)!a!}\,p_1{}^{a}(1-p_1)^{n-a}\right]$$

Re-writing this probability function in accordance with the convention we followed in the second square-bracketed expression, we have

$$P_R(m;n,p_1)$$

The Binomial Model can now be re-written in a simplified form:

$$C = SP_R(m;n,p_1) - EA^{-n}P_R(m;n,p) \qquad 13(1)$$

A DERIVATION OF THE CONTINUOUS-TIME MODEL

Continuous Compounding

The first thing to look at as we move towards a continuous-time version of the option-pricing model is the discount factor. 'A' represents $(1+r)$, where r is the discount rate expressed in percent per discrete period, compounded over each of the n discrete periods to expiration of the option. Now, rather than express r in terms of, "percent per discrete period of duration t, compounded n times over the life of the option (i.e., once each t)," we can instead express r in terms of, "percent per annum, compounded N times per annum." If T is the number of years to expiration of the option, then the number of compounding periods to expiration is NT. With this change in the meaning of 'r' our discount factor, A^{-n}, must change correspondingly, and becomes $A^{-\mathrm{NT}}$.

As the duration of each discrete period decreases towards zero, so N—the number of discrete periods in one year—increases towards infinity, and we move towards *continuous compounding* at a rate of r% p.a. If we can find the annually compounded equivalent of this continuously compounded rate of r% p.a., we can simply use the number of years to expiration of the call, T, as the number of discounting periods in our equation.

We saw in Chapter 2 how to compute discount rates or interest rates which are equivalent to those compounded over different periods. In the present case the question is, "at what rate, r_1% p.a., would I need to compound an amount, Y, over T years, such that I would receive repayment of interest and principal in an amount equal to that I would have received had I compounded it over T years of N periods per year, at a rate of r% p.a. (i.e. at a rate of r/N% per compounding period)?" In other words, for what r_1 does

$$Y(1+r_1)^{\mathrm{T}} = Y(1+r/\mathrm{N})^{\mathrm{NT}}$$

It can be shown, that as $\mathrm{N}\rightarrow\infty$ (i.e., as N tends towards infinity),

$$(1+r_1)^{\mathrm{T}} \rightarrow e^{r\mathrm{T}}$$

where e is a mathematical constant—the exponential—with a value of approximately 2.718.

Thus, in the limit:

$$A^{-\mathrm{NT}} = e^{-r\mathrm{T}} \tag{13(2)}$$

The Probability Functions

The next step on the road to the continuous-time limit requires us to look closely at the features of the pattern of price changes we invoked to derive the Binomial Model. This pattern involved two possible factors of change (u and d) over any one discrete period of time, t. This pattern is termed a *binomial random walk* and results in discrete possible price outcomes, from a low of $d^n.S$ to a high of $u^n.S$. These outcomes can be depicted graphically, on a histogram. Consider the case where $n = 4$ and the probability of a change by a factor of u is equal to that of a change by a factor of d (i.e., $p = (1\text{-}p) = ½$). The case in which $S = \$100$ and $u = 1.1$ and $d = 0.9$ is depicted in Figure 13–1, where the figures in the *Probability* column are derived from the binomial formula:

$$P_R(u^a.d^{n-a}.S) = \frac{n!}{(n-a)!a!}\, p^a(1-p)^{n-a}$$

The information contained in Figure 13–1 can be depicted on a histogram—see Figure 13–2.

As $t \rightarrow 0$ so the number of possible price outcomes $\rightarrow \infty$, and the more the graph in Figure 13–2 tends to the smooth, continuous line depicted in Figure 13–3.

One thing to notice about continuous-time probability distribution of Figure 13–3 is that it is not symmetrical,

Figure 13–1

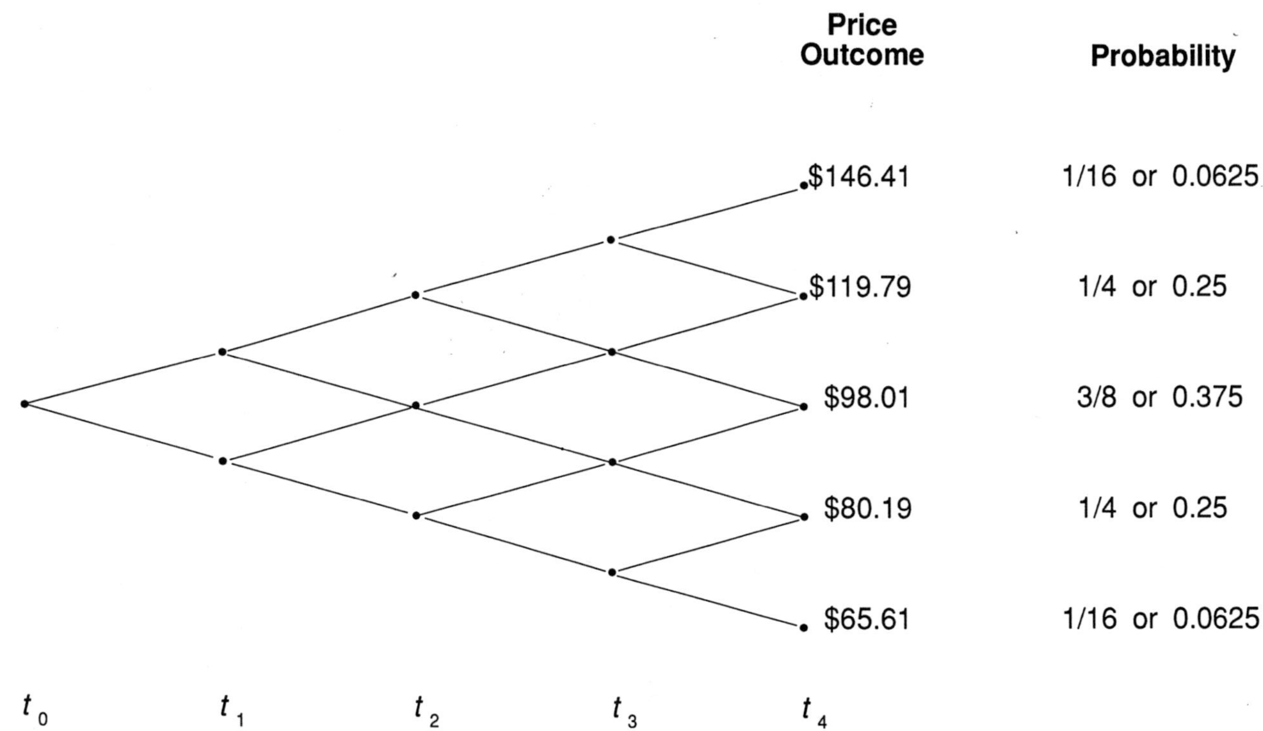

Price Outcome
Probability
$146.41
1/16 or 0.0625
$119.79
1/4 or 0.25
$98.01
3/8 or 0.375
$80.19
1/4 or 0.25
$65.61
1/16 or 0.0625
t_0
t_1
t_2
t_3
t_4

Figure 13–2

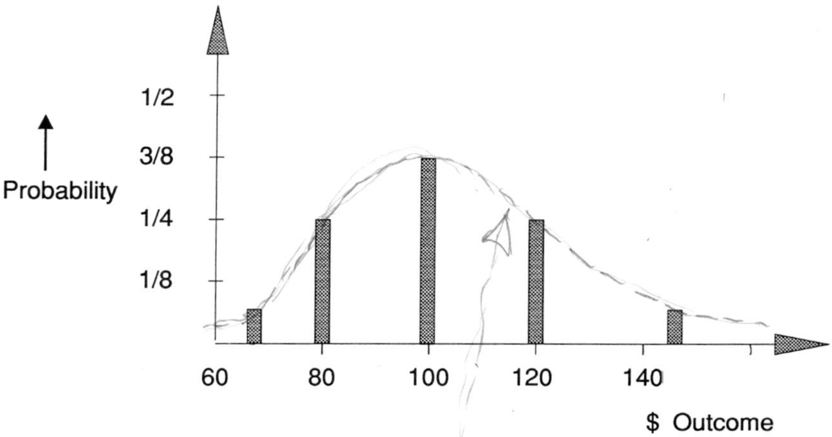

Figure 13–3

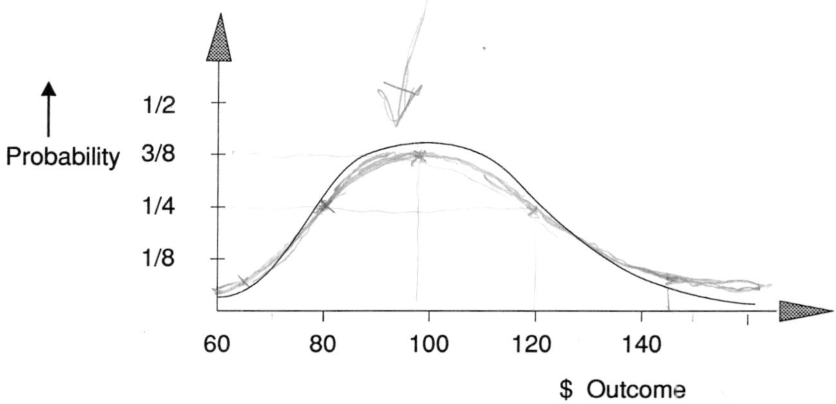

despite the fact that we have assumed $p = (1-p)$. This is because the binomial random walk, of which this is the limiting case as $t \rightarrow 0$, entails proportional moves over each period of t, rather than absolute moves. The up-step from \$110 to \$121 from t_1 to t_2 is a 10% price change, but is \$11 in absolute terms. The up-step from \$90 to \$99 in the same period is also a 10% upward price change—the same relative magnitude—but it is only \$9 in absolute terms.

While the graph of $P_R(u^a.d^{n-a}.S)$ against $u^a.d^{n-a}.S$ is not symmetrical, the graph of $P_R(u^a.d^{n-a}.S)$ against log $u^a.d^{n-a}.S$ is symmetrical; that is, log $u^a.d^{n-a}.S$ is *normally distributed* against the y-axis values.[1] This distribution is represented by the familiar bell-shaped curve. It has the quality of symmetry about the mean value of the randomly distributed variable depicted on the x-axis—log $u^a.d^{n-a}.S$—and the further quality that the mean, median and mode of that variable are all equal.

Working with the normally distributed random variable log $u^a.d^{n-a}.S$, rather than the lognormally distributed $u^a.d^{n-a}.S$, is useful because the shape and the position of the normal distribution bell curve are defined by just two measures: the mean of the random variable and the standard deviation (signified by 'σ') of the data—a measure of the dispersion of the values of the random variable about the mean. In Figure 13–4:

curves A and B have the same standard deviation but different means;

[1] If $y = m^x$ then $x = \log_m y$; expressed verbally, "x equals log y to the base m." It is the power to which the base, m, must be raised to equal y. When we refer henceforth to "log y" we will be using the natural logarithm—sometimes written "ln y"—which uses the exponential, e, as the base. Thus, if $x = \ln y$, then $y = e^x$.

As log $u^a.d^{n-a}.S$ is a normally distributed variable, so $u^a.d^{n-a}.S$ is said to be *lognormally* distributed.

Figure 13–4

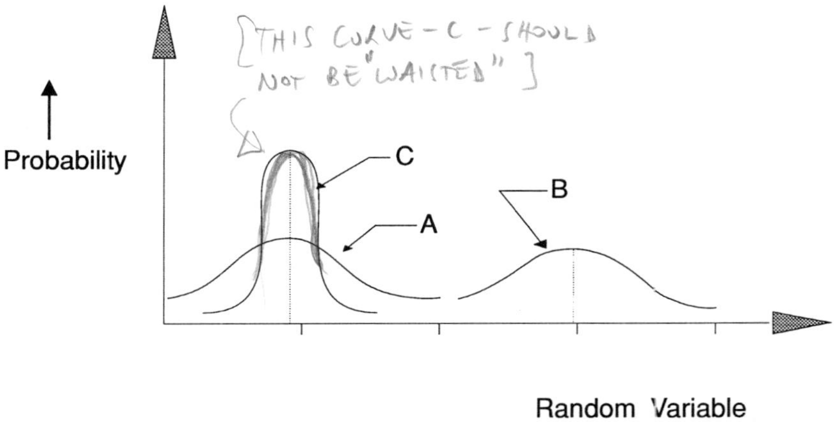

curves A and C have the same mean but different standard deviations; and

curves B and C have different standard deviations and different means.

To determine the standard deviation of a series of values of x first determine the mean of those x-values—call it μ. Second, determine the amount by which each x-value exceeds μ (i.e., find $x - \mu$ for each x-value). Obviously, x-values below μ will give negative values for $x - \mu$. To eliminate negatives, the third step is to square each $x - \mu$ value. Fourth, find the mean of these squared values, and fifth find the square root of the result:

$$\sigma = \sqrt{\sum_{q=1}^{\omega} \frac{(x_q - \mu)^2}{\omega}}$$

where

x_q is the qth x-value;

μ is the mean of the x-values; and

ω is the number of x-values in the sample.

A normal distribution bell curve is, as we have said, defined by just the mean of the data, which determines where along the x-axis the curve will peak, and the standard deviation of the data, which determines whether the curve will be tall and skinny (low standard deviation), or short and fat (high standard deviation).

Now think back to the simplified Binomial Model, Equation 13(1):

$$C = SP_R(m;n,p_1) - EA^{-n}P_R(m;n,p)$$

The $P_R(.)$ expressions, as we described, represent probability functions—in the case of $P_R(m; n,p)$, the probability of m or more moves by a factor of u, from a total of n moves, where the probability of any one move being a u-move is p. Since m was defined such that u-moves numbering more than m will mean the call option expires in-the-money, then '$P_R(m; n,p)$' represents the overall probability of the call option expiring at- or in-the-money. If we depict the logarithms of price-outcomes graphically at the continuous-time limit, using the normal distribution bell curve, then the overall probability of the call option expiring at- or in-the-money is represented by

Figure 13–5

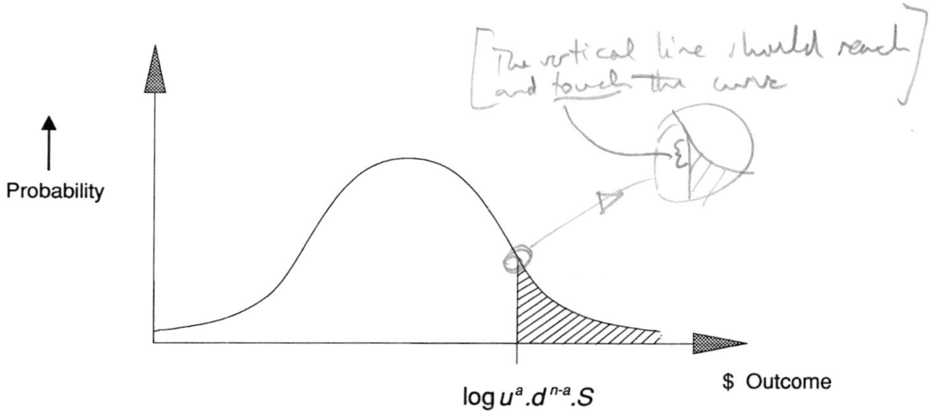

the proportion of the area under the curve to the right of the *x*-axis value corresponding to the exercise price, *E*. That is, to the right of an *x*-axis value of log *E* (see Figure 13–5).

In Figure 13–5, the overall probability of an outcome at- or in-the-money is equal to the fraction of the total area under curve that is shaded.

We can use what is called the normal density function to determine the shaded area. However, it helps first to 'standardize' the normal distribution bell curve by converting the *x*-axis values to 'Z-scores', using the transformational equation:

$$z = \frac{x - \mu}{\sigma}$$

where

x is the value of the normally distributed random variable—in our case the natural logarithm of the price outcome;

μ is the mean of the x-values; and

σ is the standard deviation of the x-values.

The benefit of using the standardized normal distribution bell curve (or the *standard normal curve*) is that it has a mean of zero and a standard deviation of 1 and enables us to make certain inferences based upon what we know about its characteristics.

The standard normal curve is described by the standard normal density function, $f_N(z)$:[2]

$$f_N(z) = \frac{1}{\sqrt{2\pi}} e^{-z^2/2}$$

The distribution of the x-axis values (i.e., the Z-scores) is given by the corresponding standard normal distrbution function, written '*N(.)*':

$$N(z_1) = \frac{1}{\sqrt{2\pi}} \int_{-\infty}^{z_1} e^{-y^2/2}\, dy$$

For some x-axis value, z_1, $N(z_1)$ represents the area under the standard normal curve from an x-axis value (i.e., Z-score)

---

[2] The density function for the normal distribution is given by

$$f(x) = \frac{1}{\sigma\sqrt{2\pi}} e^{-(x-\mu)^2/2\sigma^2} \qquad -\infty < x < \infty$$

Converting the x-values to Z-scores so that $\mu=0$ and $\sigma=1$, we obtain the standard normal density function, $f_N(.)$.

of minus infinity to z_1, i.e., the area under the standard normal curve to the left of the x-axis value of z_1. $N(z_1)$, in other words, gives us the total probability that the Z-score will take a value of less than or equal to z_1. Since the area under the entire curve from a Z-score value of minus infinity to plus infinity (i.e. the total probablity of any Z-score within those limits) is equal to one, we know that the area to the right of a Z-score of z_1 (that is, the probability of a Z-score exceeding z_1) must be $1\text{-}N(z_1)$. Moreover, from the symmetry of the standard normal curve about a mean of zero, we know that $1\text{-}N(z_1) = N(-z_1)$.

Let us now look at the expression $P_R(m;n,p)$ from the simplified Binomial Model (Equation 13(1)). This probability can be determined using the standard normal distribution function; we can compute $N(-z_2)$, where z_2 is the x-axis value corresponding to the exercise price, E, of the call option being valued. Hence, $N(-z_2)$ is the probability of a stock price outcome equal to or exceeding E:

$$P_R\,(m;n,p) = N(-z_2) \qquad 13(3)$$

Remember, we derived the standard normal curve by transforming a curve which depicted the natural logarithm of each possible price outcome along the x-axis. The transformation consisted in converting the x-axis values (log price outcome) to Z-scores using the transformational equation $z = (x-\mu)/\sigma$. Hence,

$$Z\text{-}score_k = \frac{\log \textit{price outcome}_k - \textit{mean of} \log \textit{price outcome}}{\textit{standard deviation of} \log \textit{price outcomes}}$$

and thus

$$z_2 = \frac{\log E - \textit{mean of} \log \textit{price outcomes}}{\textit{standard deviation of} \log \textit{price outcomes}}$$

With some relatively complicated mathematics it can be shown that at the continuous-time limit, as $n \rightarrow \infty$ and $t \rightarrow 0$,

$$-z_2 = \frac{1}{2\sigma\sqrt{T}}(2\ln(S/E) + 2rT - \sigma^2 T)$$

where

σ is the annual standard deviation of the price (S) of the underlying commodity;

r is the continuously-compounded interest rate, expressed in % p.a.; and

T is the time to expiration of the option in years.

Note that T is expressed in years; therefore, σ is expressed as an *annual* stanard deviation. It is the annual *volatility* of the price of the underlying commodity and must be estimated on the basis of past prices. Estimating volatility is further discussed below.

Having determined z_2 such that $N(-z_2) = P_R(m;n,p)$ we can similarly determine z_3 such that

$$N(-z_3) = P_R(m;n,p_1) \qquad 13(4)$$

Again, we can show that in the continuous-time limit

$$-z_3 = \frac{\ln(S/E) + rT}{\sigma\sqrt{T}} + \frac{\sigma\sqrt{T}}{2}$$

$$= -z_2 + \sigma\sqrt{T}$$

Hence,

$$-z_2 = -z_3 - \sigma\sqrt{T}$$

Combining Equations 13(1), 13(2), 13(3) and 13(4), we have the Black-Scholes option pricing formula for pricing calls on non-income bearing commodities:

$$C = SN(-z_3) - Ee^{-rT}N(-z_3-\sigma\sqrt{T}\,)$$

ESTIMATING VOLATILITY

Of the variables of which the call price, C, is (by the Black-Scholes model) a function, only the annual standard deviation of the price of the underlying commodity (i.e., the underlying commodity's volatility) presents a real measurement problem. We derived the model on the assumption that the possible prices of the underlying commodity are lognormally distributed. Suppose the underlying commodity is a non-dividend paying share of stock. Monday's closing price of the stock was S_M, Tuesday's was S_T, Wednesday's was S_W, and Thursday's was S_{Th}. Between Monday and Tuesday the stock price moved by an up-factor of S_T/S_M, between Tuesday and Wednesday by an up-factor of S_W/S_T, and so on.

The assumption that the possible prices of the underlying stock are lognormally distributed entails that the natural logarithms of the price up-factors are normally distributed. The standard deviation of the natural logarithms of our three up-factors—$\ln(S_T/S_M)$, $\ln(S_W/S_T)$, and $\ln(S_{Th}/S_W)$—is the *daily* volitility of the stock price, measured on the basis of our closing prices data. It is not *the only* daily volatility of the stock price, since the standard deviation we compute will or may vary with the stock price data we have at hand.

In order to compute the standard deviation above, we need to know the mean of our ln(up-factor) variables. We might simply take the mean of the three bits of data we have available to us—i.e., $(\ln(S_T/S_M)+\ln(S_W/S_T)+\ln(S_{Th}/S_W))/3$. But different samples (say the closing stock prices for Tuesday through Friday, rather than Monday through Thursday) may well have quite different means. There is a further problem, which is that even if we take the largest pool of data available to us (in this case, *every* daily up-factor by which the stock has ever moved), the estimated standard deviation thus obtained will be biased. There is, however, a technique for correcting for this bias. First, we obtain the estimated standard deviation of the series of natural logarithms of our daily up-factors about the mean of the data. Second, we square the result to give the *variance, v*, of the data. Third, we apply a correction factor. This consists in multiplying the variance by 3/(3-1), where 3 is the number of natural logarithms in the series. If we denote the unbiased daily estimated standard deviation and variance by 'σ_u' and 'v_u' respectively, then

$$v_u = v \frac{\omega}{(\omega-1)} = \sigma_u{}^2$$

Now recall the way in which we derived the standard deviation of a series of random variables, where the qth random variable is denoted by 'x_q':

$$\sigma = \sqrt{\sum_{q=1}^{\omega} \frac{(x_q-\mu)^2}{\omega}}$$

The random variable in our volitility estimator is the natural logarithm of the up-factors. Denoting the qth up-factor 'u_q' and the mean of the ω up-factors 'μ_ω' we have

$$\sigma_u{}^2 = \frac{\omega}{(\omega-1)} \sum_{q=1}^{\omega} \frac{(\ln u_q-\mu_\omega)^2}{\omega}$$

$$= \frac{1}{(\omega-1)} \sum_{q=1}^{\omega} (\ln u_q - \mu_\omega)^2$$

In the Black-Scholes model, of course, the volitility measure is the annual standard deviation of the price of the underlying commodity. In the above example, however, we estimated an unbiased *daily* volatility from the unbiased *daily* variance. The adjustment of an *n*-day variance to an *annual* variance, from which the annual volatility can be computed, is straightforward. Simply multiply the *n*-day variance by the number of *n*-day periods in one year.

Of course, volatilities change over time. In particular, the mean of the data on the basis of which we calculate the volatility may change. It can be shown, however, that the mean has only a small effect on our volatility estimation when the period between our price observations is fairly small. Be this as it may, however, the fact remains that, as we will see in the coming chapter, the possibility of a change in volatility is one exposure we will have to take into account when constructing hedges for options positions.

Implied Volatility

The foregoing hopefully brings out why it is more appropriate to talk of *estimating* volatilities than it is to talk of *measuring* volatilities. Note that a number of data and information services compute, on various bases, volatilities of a wide range of commodities, for the benefit of options traders. However, traders look more closely at one particular volatility measure than any other: *implied volatility*. To find the implied volatility of a commodity simply solve the continuous-time option pricing model for σ (i.e., for the volatility variable), rather than for C, putting the actual market price of the call option question in the place of 'C' in the model. Implied volatility, in other words, is the value for σ at which C_{actual} is equal to $C_{theoretical}$.

Clearly, using an implied volatility to compute a fair option price is circular. It is analogous to using a comparative measure such as a price-earnings ratio to value a share of stock. The valuation thus derived is only 'fair' to the extent that the prices used for the comparison are 'fair'. But implied volatility has a use. It enables the relative value of options of the same series and of the same class to be assessed. (We will see what it is for two options to be of the same series or the same class in the coming chapter.) It is important to bear in mind here, however, that many traders use a continuous-time option-pricing model such as we have derived to assess *comparative* rather than *absolute* option values.

Chapter 14

14

Use of the Continuous-Time Option Pricing Model

DELTA HEDGING

Having derived a continuous-time option pricing model, what use can we make of it? Is it an academic curiosity, telling us only something about 'fair' option prices, or are the values it suggests correct, no-arbitrage prices, deviations from which can (in a world free of transaction costs, bid-offer spreads, taxes and other economic elements omitted from our analysis) be exploited to yield riskless profits?

No! 249

In Chapter 12, we described the arbitrage pricing of call options with one period to expiration and introduced the concept of the hedge ratio (*H*). *H* was computed on the basis that the yield of a portfolio comprising *H* calls and a short forward position in one unit of the underlying commodity is equal to the riskless interest rate, whether the price of the underlying commodity at the end of the investment period turns out to be *u.S* or *d.S*. *H* is, in other words, the ratio of the spread between the possible price outcomes after one period to that between the possible values of a call on one unit of the underlying commodity at the end of the period:

$$H = \frac{S(u-d)}{C_u - C_d}$$

The sensitivity of the value of a call to a small change in the value of the underlying commodity (i.e., the reciprocal of *H*) can also be determined in the continuous-time limit. It is simply the partial derivative of the continuous-time formula with respect to *S* (i.e., $\partial C/\partial S$) and is termed the *delta* (Δ) of the call price:[1]

$$\Delta_c = \frac{1}{H}$$

and, as $n \rightarrow \infty$ and $t \rightarrow 0$, so

$$\frac{C_u - C_d}{S(u-d)} \rightarrow \frac{\partial C}{\partial S} = \Delta_c$$

[1] This should be clear. The yield on the portfolio comprising *H* calls (each on one unit of the underlying commodity) and a short forward position in one unit of the underlying commodity is equal to the riskless interest rate. At the continuous-time limit the discount factor is zero (since $t = 0$) and the break-even forward price equals the spot price of the underlying commodity. Hence the rise in price of *H* calls less the rise in price of one unit of the underlying commodity is equal to zero: $H.\delta_C - \delta_S = 0$.

Using the Black-Scholes formula and differentiating with respect to S, it can be shown that $\partial C/\partial S = N(-z_3)$. In other words, all else remaining equal, for a small rise, g, in the price of the underlying commodity, the call price will rise by $gN(-z_3)$.

We can use the delta to construct a *delta hedge* by which we can hope to profit from, for example, the mispricing of an option. Suppose you use the continuous-time model to determine that the exchange-traded International Widget April 1990 $90 call (that is, the call expiring in April 1990 and having an exercise price of $90 per share for the 100 underlying shares) is overpriced. Its 'theoretical' value is $3 per underlying share, while it is in fact currently selling for $5 per underlying share. The option delta is 0.3. To profit from the mispricing, an arbitrageur could sell three calls and hedge his exposure with the purchase of ninety Widget shares.[2] However, one week later the Widget stock price has moved, such that the delta of the option has changed to 0.5. To remain *delta neutral* and unexposed to price moves in the stock the arbitrageur must now re-weight his portfolio. From being short three calls and long ninety shares he must move to a position of being long one hundred and fifty shares.

This illustrates a couple of points of potential exposure. For one thing, the delta of an option is the *instantaneous* rate of change in the price of the option, relative to a change in the price of the underlying commodity. For each and every change in S the delta of the option will change. To remain

[2] $\Delta_c = 1/H = 0.3$. Thus, $H = 10/3$. By the definition of the hedge ratio, H, we know that for an instantaneous change in the value of the underlying shares a portfolio comprising H calls changes in value by an amount equal to one comprising 100 of the underlying shares (the number of shares underlying one exchange-traded call). Hence we need to hedge a short position in 10/3 calls with a long position in 100 of the underlying shares. Three short calls must thus be hedged using along position in 90 of the underlying shares.

fully delta-hedged the arbitrageur must instantaneously re-weight the hedge portfolio. Moreover, the call price is not just a function of S. It is also a function of other variables that may, or do change over time: the interest rate, the volatility of the price of the underlying commodity, and the time to expiration (these variables each occur in the delta function, $N(-z_3)$). Running a delta-neutral hedge using a portfolio of calls and shares is a task of Gordian complexity if exactitude is required—even assuming the continuous-time model is derived from valid assumptions embodied in, for example, the mathematical description of the stochastic process that is the change in S over time. That such assumptions are indeed valid is, as we will discuss, by no means clear.

You may now be tempted to believe that nobody would ever be brave enough to try to arbitrage mispriced options. In fact, people do, and it is considerably easier than the forego-ing might suggest. The aim in arbitraging options—or any-thing else for that matter—is, as we have seen, to construct a portfolio whose net price is immune from changes in the price of the underlying commodity and/or in other variables. That is, if part of the portfolio (V_1) rises in price by g then the rest of the portfolio—the hedge (V_2)—falls in value by g. It is delta-neutral because this offsetting quality can be expressed:

$$\Delta V_1 = -\Delta V_2$$

Hence,

$$\Delta V_1 + \Delta V_2 = 0$$

where $\Delta V_1 + \Delta V_2$ is the delta of the portfolio, sometimes termed the *position delta*. Suppose that V_1 is a position in h_c calls (i.e., $V_1 = h_c C$) and is hedged with h_x X-type securities (i.e., $V_2 = h_x X$). The position delta in this case is $h_c \Delta_c + h_x \Delta_x$.

ELASTICITY

Closely related to the delta of an option position is the *elasticity* of the position—a measure of the *proportional* change in the position value, relative to a change in the price of the underlying commodity. It is simply the product of the position delta and $S/(V_1+V_2)$ and is measured by the lambda (Λ) of the position:

$$\Lambda_{position} = \Delta_{position} \frac{S}{(V_1+V_2)}$$

At this point, it should be clear that we are not limited to hedging any option position with a position in the underlying commodity. We could hedge it with anything whose value is largely a function of S, so long as we achieve the desired offsetting characteristic: $h_c\Delta_c = - h_x\Delta_x$. To hedge the sale of International Widget's April 1990 $90 calls, for example, we might use—as the X-type security—a long position in relatively cheaper (correctly priced or underpriced) July 1990 $90 calls, April 1990 $100 calls, a short position in April 1990 $90 puts, or a long position in the stock itself.

GAMMA, THETA AND KAPPA

Selection of the commodity with which to hedge an option should be guided by some obvious and fundamental principles. First, the hedge security should not be mispriced in the same way as the option being hedged. It is no good selling overpriced April 1990 $90 calls only to give back the potential profit by hedging with, say, a long position in the similarly overpriced April 1990 $95 calls. Second, the best hedge portfolio will be the one that requires re-weighting as little as possible as S changes. One of the arbitrageur's targets, in other words, is to keep the position delta as close to zero as possible for changes in S, in order that a small change in S to which he fails to respond will not wipe him out. The rate of change of the position delta with respect to S is termed the *sensitivity ratio*, or *gamma* (Γ) of the position:

$$\Gamma_{position} = \frac{\partial(\Delta_{position})}{\partial S}$$

$$= h_c\left(\frac{\partial \Delta_c}{\partial S}\right) + h_x\left(\frac{\partial \Delta_x}{\partial S}\right)$$

$$= h_c\Gamma_c + h_x\,\Gamma_x$$

By the delta and gamma definitions, $\Gamma_c = \partial(\partial C/\partial S)/\partial S$. The gamma of a call (and of a position) is, in other words, a measure of the sensitivity of the call's (position's) delta to changes in the price of the underlying commodity; hence, it is a measure of the sensitivity of the call's (position's) *value* to the *variability* of the price of the underlying commodity.

Third, the position value is also a function of variables other than S, and the best hedge will be that for which the position value is least sensitive to changes in these other variables. The influence of the passing of *time* on the value of a position is measured by the position *theta* (Θ). As we saw in Chapter 9, the passing of time (a decrease in T) will normally be reflected by a movement in the same direction—a decrease—in the value (C) of a call and the value (P) of a put. Calls and puts are said to have *negative* time bias. Thus,

$$\Theta_{call} = -\frac{\partial C}{\partial T}$$

$$\Theta_{put} = -\frac{\partial P}{\partial \mathrm{T}}$$

and

$$\Theta_{position} = -\frac{\partial(V_1+V_2)}{\partial \mathrm{T}}$$

$$= -\frac{\partial(h_c C+h_x X)}{\partial \mathrm{T}}$$

The influence of a change in the *volatility* of the underlying commodity on the value of a position is measured by the position *kappa* (K):

$$K_{position} = -\frac{\partial(V_1+V_2)}{\partial \sigma}$$

A position with a kappa of zero will not change in price (that it, its *theoretical* price will not change) with a change in the volatility of the underlying commodity.

So far we have looked briefly at some of the considerations involved in hedging for riskless arbitrage profits. Note that the measures of Δ, Λ, Γ, Θ and K are also useful tools in constructing positions to manage or exploit anticipated moves or trends in the variables of which the position value is a function. For example, suppose you are bullish on a stock and expect its price to rise. You are constructing a position to hedge a mispriced call in the stock but want to structure the position to rise in value with the anticipated rise in *S*. The position will not be delta-neutral but delta-positive:

$$h_c\Delta_c+h_x\Delta_x > 0$$

In this case, as S rises, V_1 (i.e., h_cC) rises in value more than V_2 (i.e., h_xX) falls in value—that is, the position value rises. Conversely, if you expect the stock price to fall you would construct a delta-negative position.

By the same token, a position with a negative gamma might be constructed in order to profit from an anticipated period of increased variability in the price of the underlying commodity, while a position with a positive kappa might be constructed to profit from an anticipated increase in the implied volatility at which options on the underlying commodity trade. A detailed exposition of these strategies is, however, beyond the scope of this chapter. Rather, we turn to a brief analysis of some of the more common options trading strategies.

BASIC OPTIONS TRADING STRATEGIES

Options trading strategies can be classified into one or other of four types:

(i) Uncovered or Naked Positions

are those in which an option is purchased or sold (written) without any offsetting position being held in another option or in the underlying commodity itself. Thus, purchasing an April $110 IBM call without simultaneously carrying a short position in IBM stock will constitute a naked long call position.

(ii) Covered Positions

(sometimes referred to as *hedged* positions) combine options with an offsetting position in the underlying commodity or in another option. A long position in IBM stock along with a short IBM call position, for example, is a covered or hedged position.

(iii) Spread Positions

are those in which a long position in an option is held alongside a short position in an option of the same *class* but a different *series*. Options are said to be of the same class when they are all of the same type (i.e., all calls or all puts) *and* have the same underlying commodity. Options of the same class may have different expirations and strike prices. Options of the same class which also have the same expiration and strike price, however, are said to be of the same series. Thus, the purchase of a September 250 S&P 100 Index call, coupled with the sale of a September 260 S&P 100 Index call comprises a spread position. Specifically, this is a *vertical* or *price spread* position because the options involved are the same except for their strike prices. A *horizontal* or *calendar spread* would be one in which the options had the same strike prices but different expirations. A *diagonal spread* position is one in which the options are of the same class but have different strike prices *and* different expirations.

(iv) Combination Positions

are those containing an option of one type (i.e., a call or a put) alongside an option on the same underlying commodity but of different type, where the options comprising the position are either both purchased or both sold. Combination positions may be long positions, in which both options are purchased, or short positions, in which both are sold. A combination involving options with the same expiration and strike price is termed a *straddle*. Thus, a combination position comprising a short April $110 IBM call and a short April $110 IBM put is a straddle.

Chapter 15

15

Debt and Equity Securities as Options

COMPARATIVE VERSUS ABSOLUTE VALUATION TECHNIQUES

The reflective, aging investment banker (who was approaching forty-two) reminded his audience that, "in my day we valued securities using measures like price/earnings ratios and yields. We simply made comparisons among various issues in our search for bargains; we had no need of complicated theory."

Times change, however, and since the investment banker's day simple ratios and comparative analyses have been of declining utility in the pricing of debt and equity securities.

This is in part because the wave of leveraged buyouts of the mid to late 1980s left many formerly comparable companies looking very different in terms of their capital structures, making it difficult for analysts confidently to make inferences based on comparisons among them. But there is also a grave theoretical limitation to which comparative valuations are subject. In order for an investor or investment banker to identify bargains—and thus to exploit the implied profit potential—he must know which of a pool of comparable but non-aligned stocks is *mis*priced. Suppose that there exist seven comparable oil company stocks. Six of the seven are priced closely together, while the seventh, company A, is trading at a substantially lower earnings multiple. It may be unlikely, but it is not inconceivable, that company A is in fact 'correctly' priced and that the other six will soon be trading down to A's level. The investment banker's comparative pricing methodology will not tell him the direction of mispricing, it will only suggest[1] that *some* mispricing exists.

In all financial valuation the one and *only* fundamental and objective yardstick the analyst has at his disposal is the riskless interest rate. It is against the riskless interest rate that all investment values are measured. This truth can be glimpsed as soon as we begin in search of an absolute valuation of a debt security. If International Widget Corporation issues ten-year bonds, the upper bound to the possible fair value of the bonds will clearly be the price at which they confer a yield equal to the riskless ten-year interest rate. Why should anyone (anyone, that is, who fails to perceive value in losing money) assume the risk associated with them without potential compensation? The question of bond valuation, therefore, reduces to the question whether the potential compensation attributable to the assumption of risk (i.e., the

1 "Suggest" because who is to say that there is not, in fact, a *relevant difference* to account for non-alignment?

spread between the bond's prospective yield to maturity and the riskless interest rate) fairly reflects the amount of that risk.

CAPITAL SECURITIES AS OPTIONS

The spread between the riskless interest rate and the rate at which a particular company borrows—known as the company's borrowing *margin* or *spread*—reflects the probability of the company defaulting on its obligation. It is, in other words, compensation paid to the investor in consideration of the possibility of default. If a company does default on its obligations, its lenders typically are able to force a bankruptcy and ultimately, perhaps, to force the company into liquidation. But suppose the lenders choose never to take advantage of this ability. Instead, suppose they are content to receive in any year (j) the higher of either the amount contractually due to them (call it I_j) or the maximum amount the company can *afford* to pay (i.e. the company's cash flow which is available for debt service—call it CF_j). If CF_j is less than or equal to I_j then the entirety of that cash flow is allocable to the lenders. If, however, CF_j exceeds I_j the lenders are paid in full and the balance of the cash flow (CF_j - I_j) is paid to or reinvested for the benefit of shareholders and the Internal Revenue Service (IRS). Shareholders and the IRS, in other words, receive (directly or indirectly) the higher of CF_j - I_j and zero, or

$$max(CF_j - I_j, 0)$$

This expression simply represents the payoff of a long call position, where the value of the underlying commodity is CF_j and the exercise price is I_j. It is, in other words, as though the lenders *own* the cash flows of the company in each year, but have sold a call on each of those cash flows to shareholders and the IRS, the exercise price of which is equal to the amount of interest due. If we signify the value of this call by '$C1_j$' we thus have a way of expressing the pre-tax equity value of the company:

$$\textit{Pre–tax equity value} = \sum_{j=1}^{\infty} C1_j \qquad 15(1)$$

This analysis is crude and approximate insofar as it takes no account either of the lenders' ability to force bankruptcy or liquidation or of the cumulative aspect of debt obligations, whereby lenders are entitled to receive late payments with interest on the overdue amounts. The analysis is, however, serviceable for our purposes given the complication of a capricious and unpredictable bankruptcy system.[2]

ASSESSING THE VALUE OF THE FIRM

The aggregate value of the capital securities of any company consists in the aggregate present value of the cash flows allocable to the holders of those securities. Using the terminology introduced above, call the cash flow allocable to capital securities in year j 'CF_j'. Now we can break CF_j down into parts, as follows:

$$CF_j = max(CF_j–E_j, 0) – max(E_j–CF_j, 0) + E_j$$

where E_j is any number.

The first '*max*' expression on the right side of the equality should be readily recognizable as representing the payoff of a long call on CF_j with an exercise price of E_j, while the second

---

[2] A refinement of the analysis might include a portrayal of the uncertainty associated with the outcome of bankruptcy proceedings as a series of bets exchanged among the various parties to those proceedings. The refinement itself will be left to the reader.

expression represents the payoff of a short (because the expression is negative) put on CF_j, again with an exercise price of E_j. If we signify the value of the call by '$C2_j$' and that of the put by 'P_j', we will have a simple means of expressing the present value of the entitlement to CF_j; it is simply the sum of the component long call and short put positions and E_j, i.e., $C2_j - P_j + E_j$. Hence the value of the capital securities of the company, being equal to the aggregate of the present values of CF_j for $j = 1$ to $j = \infty$, can be simply expressed:

$$\textit{Value of capital securities} = \sum_{j=1}^{\infty} (C2_j - P_j + E_j) \qquad 15(2)$$

We can now derive the value of the debt securities of the company. The debt value is equal to the capital value less the pre-tax equity value of the firm, hence, using Equations 15(1) and 15(2):

$$\textit{Value of debt securities} = \sum_{j=1}^{\infty} (C2_j - P_j + E_j - C1_j) \quad 15(3)$$

The value of debt securities is expressed in Equation 15(3) as a function of three component option values. But the value of any option is not, by the option pricing formulae derived in earlier chapters, a function of any interest rate other than the riskless rate. Hence, by Equation 15(3) we have a means of valuing debt securities other than by reference to a 'risky' discount rate. The appropriate 'risky' discount rate may itself be derived as a function of the value of debt securities suggested by Equation 15(3) and the payments due in respect of those debt securities. The actual derivation is, for any real-world situation, highly complex. The conceptual analysis is, however, of very great importance for we have proved that proper borrowing margins do not materialize from thin air but spring from, ultimately, the gaming analysis which lies behind the option pricing models.

BANKS AS OPTIONS SPECULATORS

The conclusion that corporate debt obligations may be analyzed in terms of options has very important and practical implications, as the following case should serve to show. It is accepted wisdom that banks should not lend to corporations at fixed rates of interest if they (the banks) borrow at floating rates of interest. Lending to a company at a fixed rate of, say, 9% p.a. for a ten-year period may look wonderfully profitable today, when the bank is borrowing at, say, 7½% p.a. But it looks disastrous when, four years down the road, that borrowing rate has risen to 10% p.a. Hence, banks have established huge *interest rate swap* businesses by which they match their fixed rate entitlements with their fixed rate obligations and their floating rate entitlements with their floating rate obligations. By this means, they match their assets to their liabilities and eliminate interest rate risk, right? *Wrong.*

Consider the following scenarios:

> *Scenario 1*: Third Bank of Firston makes a $10 million loan to International Widget Corporation. The loan has a five-year bullet maturity and an interest rate of Prime+1% p.a., adjustable every six months. Third Bank funds the loan by borrowing five year funds at a similarly adjustable interest rate of Prime+¼ % p.a.
>
> *Scenario 2*: Third Bank of Firston makes a $10 million loan to International Widget Corporation. The loan has a five-year bullet maturity and a fixed interest

> rate of 9% p.a. Third Bank funds the loan by issuing five-year bonds at a cost of 8¼% p.a.

Now consider what happens if after just one year International Widget becomes insolvent and is liquidated:

> *Scenario 1*: Third Bank of Firston mercifully is repaid in full. It uses the $10 million it receives by way of the liquidation to repay its floating rate loan in full.
>
> *Scenario 2*: Third Bank of Firston mercifully is repaid in full. But interest rates have fallen substantially over the past year. Third Bank is unable to buy back its bonds, except at a hefty premium to the $10 million received from the Widget liquidation. If it lends the $10 million received from the liquidation to another customer, rather than using it to repurchase its bonds, it is able to do so only at a much lower rate of interest. Either way, Third Bank realizes a substantial loss.

Under Scenario 2 the amount of Third Bank's loss will be a function of then prevailing four-year interest rates. The amount of this loss—and the gain Third Bank would have realized had interest rates fallen—can be analyzed in terms of option payoffs. If the principal amount of the bonds is B and their market value is M, the amount of Third Bank's payoff is $B - M$, or $[max(B - M, 0) - max(M - B, 0)]$. This represents the payoff of a long put position plus a short call position. The underlying commodity in the case of both options is the loan (value M) and the exercise price of each is B.

By lending at a fixed rate of interest Third Bank has effectively sold a call option on its loan to International Widget and has simultaneously bought a put option on the loan. The exercise price of both the call and the put is equal to the principal amount of the loan, and both options are exercisable automatically at such time as International Widget is liquidated. If, at the time of liquidation, interest rates are down substantially—as in Scenario 2 above—then the loan value rises, the call is in-the-money, and Third Bank (as seller of the call) is out-of-pocket. If, on the other hand, interest rates are up substantially at the time of liquidation, then Third Bank (as owner of the put) realizes a windfall gain. It can either repay its funding at a discount or it can re-lend the funds at the higher prevailing rate of interest.

In Chapter 9, we derived the put-call parity equation for relating the value of a European put on a commodity to that of a European call (with the same expiration and the same exercise price) on the same commodity. The value of the short call embedded in a bank's fixed rate loan to a customer will often equal that of the embedded long put. However, banks and bank regulators should be well aware that when they (banks) involve themselves in fixed rate lending—even on a carefully matched basis—they are involving themselves inextricably and inevitably in options speculation.

Chapter 16

16

An Appraisal of the Option Pricing Models: Three Sources of Doubt

A CLOSER LOOK AT PROBABILITY

Business managers spend a great deal of time in contingency planning—insuring themselves in case things should go against them in the future. Property insurance is one of the more obvious examples of this kind of contingency planning—taking steps to mitigate the effects of, for example, a plant fire at some point in the future. The financial manager, more than most of his line colleagues—expends particular efforts in securing the foundations of the business against downturns or disasters. He does this by hedging with contingent contracts—instruments that will afford a positive payoff only if certain future events obtain. If those future events obtain, he then calculates the payoff of the contingent contract will be sufficient to offset or mitigate the losses to which the events would give rise.

Suppose that a large multinational company with substantial exports to France wants to hedge against a large depreciation in the value of the French franc, which would have the dual impact of making its French franc revenues less valuable when switched back into dollars and, as the company raises its prices in France to compensate, making its goods ultimately less competitive in the French marketplace. One strategy the company might use to mitigate this exposure is the purchase of French franc puts. If the French franc stays strong against the dollar, so much the better. True, the puts, if they were purchased slightly out-of-the-money, would expire worthless, but the company's French franc revenues would have remained strong or increased in dollar value. If the French franc falls in value, however, the puts will be exercised. Thus, whatever the market value of the franc, the company knows that by exercising its puts it can at least get an exchange rate equal to their exercise price, and it knows that it may possibly achieve a better rate, if the franc appreciates.

Put options are very much like insurance policies in that they can offset some or all of the potential losses that would be sustained if future events go against you, while leaving you with the opportunity to benefit if events go in your favor. Like fire insurance, you may suppose, the cost of this 'downside protection' will depend upon the amount insured and the risks surrounding whatever is being insured. If an insurer and a policyholder have a dispute over the premium cost of fire insurance, the two parties will normally negotiate, with the policyholder trying to convince the insurer that the probability of fire damage is lower than the insurer may be disposed to believe. If he cannot, however, *prove* that the probability is low, and in the end the two parties may reach an impasse, with the policyholder having to look elsewhere for less expensive coverage.

Insofar as there may be a wide—and legitimate—divergence in people's assessment of the risk or probability of fire damage, it follows that there may be a wide—and legitimate—divergence of views over what premium to charge. Now it follows from the claim that there is no room for a divergence of views over the correct price of an option (which is analogous to an insurance premium) that there is no room for a wide and legitimate divergence in people's assessment of the probability of a particular price outcome for the underlying commodity. This suggests that some probability assessments *are* objective.

And, indeed, this seems at first sight plausible, for while on the question of the probability of fire damage there may be room for a legitimate divergence of views, on the question of the probability of throwing a three on a roll of a die there would, surely, be a general consensus among rational people. But is this apparent objectivity illusory? This is crucial to the question, "what does option theory *really tell us* about 'correct' option values (and hence the viability of options arbitrage and hedge strategies)?" The probability distributions we invoke to describe future price outcomes associated with the underlying commodity are at the heart of option pricing models; the logical integrity (as opposed to the practical usefulness) of the models, and particularly any claim to objectivity made on their behalf, rests upon the logic of the implied probability statements.

Statements by which we assert the probability of an event typically derive from relative frequency analyses. That is, the probability of an event, A, being the outcome of a particular situation is the frequency with which A has been the outcome in the past, relative to the total number of outcomes that have occurred in the past. For example, suppose I have thrown a die 240 times and have noted the results of each throw. Now I want to determine the probability of throwing a three next time around. The crude relative frequency view suggests that the probability is the frequency with which I have thrown a three in the past, relative to the total number of past throws. Thus, if past throws have included 40 throws of a 3, the probability of a three being thrown next time is 40/240, or 16⅔%, or one-sixth.

But suppose of my 240 previous throws a three has turned up on 60 occasions, rather than 40. Does this mean the probability of throwing a 3 is ¼? Of course not. We do not measure relative frequencies by looking at *just* this die or *just* these 240 throws. We look at relative frequencies over centuries of die games. Indeed, we can go further. Over centuries of throwing cubes and all sorts of other regular, evenly-balanced solids we have come to learn that there is no reason to suppose that any one face is more likely to be thrown than any other. And it is this reference to a "reason to suppose"—embodied in what is often termed the *principle of indifference*—that is important. In recent years many probability theorists have come to ask (rhetorically) what is a probability assessment over and above an expression of one's confidence—the strength of one's reason to suppose—that this will be the case, rather than that will be the case? Their answer is: nothing.

Put another way, many theorists—propensity theorists, as they are termed—would have it that probability statements convey no information beyond information concerning the speaker's beliefs. Such statements certainly do not directly convey any information about past occurrences. For example, "the probability of throwing a three on this role of the die is one-sixth," is not simply another way of saying, "through all the [known] history of die throwing, the number three has been thrown on one-sixth of all throws." Neither is it a way of saying something about the future, such as, "of the coming x throws of this die, a three *will* be thrown $x/6$ times." For (among other problems) what number is x to be?

To say, "the probability of throwing a three, or any other particular face, on this role of the die is one-sixth," is simply, for the propensity theorist, to say, "I am no more confident that a three will be thrown than I am that any other particular face will be thrown." The subject of the utterance is not a particular face of the die, nor a pool of past or future events, nor a 'probability' (whatever peculiar sort of an entity we might care to think of a 'probability' as being). The subject is, rather, the speaker, and what is predicated of him is that he has a particular belief or set of beliefs. It follows that probability statements can be determined to be true or false only insofar as the speaker can be determined to have or not to have certain beliefs. To determine the truth of a statement about the likelihood of a three being thrown in a die game you need not go off and try throwing a die. All you need to do is to question the speaker about what beliefs he holds. And to determine whether he does or does not hold a particular belief about the outcome of a die game it may well be helpful to determine whether such a belief would be reasonable. And to determine whether such a belief would be reasonable would indeed (generally) necessitate reviewing the outcomes of die throws through history.

Equipped with the conviction that it is reasonable to have equal confidence in (or to ascribe an equal probability to) each of the six possible outcomes of a throw of a die we can compute the probability of throwing a three. The six possible outcomes are mutually exclusive and exhaustive (we will neglect the tiny probability of the die landing and balancing on an edge). The aggregate of the probability of throwing a one, plus the probability of throwing a two, and so on, up to the probability of throwing a six, must therefore be one. That six equal probabilities aggregate one entails that each probability is one-sixth.

The reason we have consensus in the matter of die game probabilities is that we are dealing with a straightforward situation in which we can readily identify the exhaustive list of possible outcomes and for which we have a large pool of past experiences on which to draw. Dealing with the probability of fire damage or, more pertinently, of share price outcomes, however, is much more complex. It is very difficult for us to remember and extrapolate from past experiences, with all their unique features, in order to predict the future. It is this sort of difference in *complexity* which accounts for one set of probability ascriptions appearing more objective than another set.

THE IMPACT OF PRICE PATH ASSUMPTIONS

Aside from the question of probability ascriptions there is another important feature of the die game which appears to set it apart from projecting share price outcomes. This is the ability under certain circumstances to hedge bets in a very simple manner. In Chapter 7, we showed that offering odds of, say, 10 to one on the throw of a three in a die game would give rise to a potential for riskless profit, so long as the aggregate of odds on all six faces were less than one. This is because we could then cover all possible outcomes of the throw for a total stake which is less than the prize money which we would be assured of winning. In the case of a share price outcome, however, we can only structure replicating positions and use arbitrage pricing to derive fair stakes for bets (as embodied in an option) by limiting the range of possible outcomes. In evolving the Binomial Pricing Model, we limited price outcomes over period t to two possibilities: one representing a change by a factor of u, the other representing a change by a factor of d. In the real world, however, such constraints cannot explain or describe important features of stock price paths. When we are projecting stock price outcomes at the end of a period, t, we simply do not have a finite and exhaustive range of mutually exclusive possible outcomes known to us. No matter how small we make t, even as we approach the limiting case—that is, as $t \to 0$—the binomial path assumption (and the diffusion process which is its continuous-time limiting case) cannot exactly describe real-world price moves. Such moves may involve jumps—discontinuities in the price path—as when new material information comes to the attention of the market.

The implication of this shortcoming of our price path assumptions is that we cannot use the Binomial Pricing Model—or its continuous-time limiting case—to give rise to absolutely watertight arbitrage strategies by which we can profit from mispricing. Cox and Ross, among others, have modified the continuous-time model to embody an assumed price path which provides for both jump and diffusion processes. Although such refinements may be useful (and, in practical terms, it is arguable whether they really do represent material advances), the fundamental problem remains. Each and every trade in a commodity takes place at a price which is in some sense logically independent of the prices at which all previous trades have taken place and at which all future trades will take place. Statistical distributions may be more or less useful in describing trends and predicting the future. But the models which embody such statistical distributions, and the predictions that flow from them, have the same logical status as political polls and predictions based on the polls. They are interesting and they are the best sort of indicators we can hope for, but in the end, if the real world turns out to conflict with the model's predictions, nobody can claim that there has been a violation of any rule of law.

MARGINAL UTILITY

There is a third reason for questioning the inviolability of option pricing theory, and this has to do with aspects of human psychology of which the theory takes no account. It has to do with the relationship which lies at the very heart of option pricing models—the basic price-payoff relationship, and whether this is a relationship that we can rely upon as accurately describing investor behavior and propensity.

To justify the idea that the fair value of a bet on a particular future event is a function of the prize which is at stake and the probability of winning (however such probability may be determined), we had—in Chapter 7—to invoke the concept of 'fairness'. The implication is that the basic price-payoff relationship has a logical status which falls short of a natural law; it enables us to derive the 'fair' price for a bet, not the one-and-only *right* price (what if people choose not to be fair?). The important question for the options trader who constructs positions to benefit from the mispricing of an option is whether options—and bets in general—*do* tend to fetch their fair prices in the open market. Disturbingly, for both the theoretician and the arbitrageur, the answer is, "only very rarely, in the simplest cases."

Consider the case of the state lottery. Just about everyone who buys a lottery ticket realizes that the basic price-payoff relationship is being violated. The lottery is a fund-raising mechanism for the state. The aggregate of prize money is less than the aggregate of stakes put up; it entails a riskless arbitrage for the state—a great business if you can get it! Since the general public, *as a body*, is bound to lose in the lottery, why does the general public play? The answer is that human nature appears to be such that we have a disposition towards the throw-away bet, or the long-shot. After all, a lottery ticket costs only a small amount. The cost of the ticket represents the buyer's downside risk. For his small outlay the buyer *could* (however unlikely) win, say, $10,000,000. This potential payoff represents his upside potential. Of course the odds are weighted heavily against him, but what is the real difference if the odds are ten million to one against or fifteen million to one against? Those are throw-away numbers and have, generally, a minimal impact on the propensity of individuals to buy lottery tickets at a particular price. The odds are, in a sense, meaningless to the betting public. The fact is that to most betting individuals, the long-shot has what is called a high *marginal utility*.

Marginal utility serves to distort many of the markets in bets and analogous commodities, including options and other financial securities. At the track, rank outsiders tend to be overbet relative to strong favorites. In the financial markets, deep out-of-the-money options tend to be overvalued relative to their in-the-money cousins. And high-growth stocks are often overvalued, particularly at their initial public offering, relative to more pedestrian issues. Leverage—the opportunity to win big for a small stake—appears to have a value all its own, more readily explainable in terms of human nature and our built-in optimism that it is in terms of arbitrage potential or fairness.

And so you might ask whether the option pricing methodology that has been evolved through this book is of any value after all. For at its heart lies an assumption that appears to fail to describe behavior in the real world. Well, the answer to that question is to be found at the very outset of this book. In Chapter 1, it was pointed out that we set out to throw light on the principles of sound and rational pricing in the securities markets. We did not set out with the aim of evolving a watertight system for playing and winning in the investment game. So, while you may harbor a lingering disappointment over the fact that untold wealth may still elude you, take heart that you have (hopefully) enhanced your ability to make rational decisions, and this should give you a meaningful edge in a highly competitive world.

FURTHER READING

(1) F. Black and M. Scholes: "The Pricing of Options and Corporate Liabilities," *Journal of Political Economy,* 81 (May-June 1973), 637-654

(2) R. Bookstaber: *Option Pricing and Investment Strategies,* revised ed. (Chicago, IL: Probus, 1987)

(3) R. Brealey and S. Myers: *Principles of Corporate Finance,* 3rd ed. (New York, NY: McGraw-Hill, 1988)

(4) M. Brenner (ed.): *Option Pricing* (Lexington, MA: D. C. Heath, 1983)

(5) E. Brigham and L. Gapenski: *Financial Management, Theory and Practice,* 5th ed. (Orlando, FL: The Dryden Press, 1988)

(6) J. Cox and M. Rubinstein: *Options Markets* (Englewood Cliffs, NJ: Prentice-Hall, 1985)

(7) D. Emanuel: "Warrant Valuation and Exercise Strategy," *Journal of Financial Economics,* 12 (August 1983), 211-236

(8) F. Fabozzi and G. Kipnis (eds.): *The Handbook of Stock Index Futures and Options* (Homewood, IL: Dow-Jones Irwin, 1989)

(9) J. Ingersoll: "A Contingent Claims Valuation of Convertible Securities," *Journal of Financial Economics,* 4 (1977)

(10) R. Jarrow and A. Rudd: *Option Pricing* (Homewood, IL: Irwin, 1983)

(11) R.C. Merton: "Theory of Rational Option Pricing," *Bell Journal of Economics and Management Science,* 4 (Spring 1973), 141-183

- "On the Pricing of Corporate Debt: The Risk Structure of Interest Rates," *Journal of Finance,* 29 (May 1974)

(12) W.F. Sharpe: *Investments,* 2nd ed. (Englewood Cliffs, NJ: Prentice-Hall, 1981)

In (3), (5) and (12) are to be found applications of discounted cash flow analysis not covered in this book. (1) is the article which laid the foundations of modern option theory. Robert Merton's two articles, (11), have also been influential; the second shows how option theory applies to risky debt. (4) contains some interesting articles, including Brealey, Hodges and Selby's "The Risk of Bank-Loan Portfolios." (2) is an easy-to-understand and comprehensive introduction to both option theory and options trading strategies. (6) is one of the most complete and comprehensive reviews of option theory and goes substantially further than the current book.

Index